F4U CORSAIR

in detail & scale

Bert Kinzey

COPYRIGHT © 1998 BY DETAIL & SCALE, INC.

All rights reserved. No part of this publication may be reproduced in any form, stored in a retrieval system, or transmitted by any means, electronic, mechanical, or otherwise, except in a review, without the written consent of the publisher.

This book is a product of Detail & Scale, Inc., which has sole responsibility for its content and layout, except that all contributors are responsible for the security clearance and copyright release of all materials submitted. Published by Squadron/Signal Publications, 1115 Crowley Drive, Carrollton, Texas 75011.

CONTRIBUTORS AND SOURCES:

Larry Webster
Lloyd Jones
Jim Roeder
Keith Ward
Paul Varga
Clark Macomber
Paul Gold

Jim Galloway
J. C. Bahr
Keith Liles
Walt Fink
Dave Pluth
Stan Parker

Vought
National Archives
U. S. Navy
U. S. Marine Corps
National Museum of Naval Aviation, Pensacola, Florida
U. S. Marine Corps Museum, Quantico, Virginia
Eagle Editions, Ltd.

Detail & Scale, Inc. and the author extend a very special word of thanks to Hill Goodspeed of the National Museum of Naval Aviation at Pensacola, Florida, and Mike Starn of the Marine Corps Museum at Quantico, Virginia. Their assistance and cooperation contributed significantly to this publication.

Many photographs in this publication are credited to their contributors. Photographs with no credit indicated were taken by the author.

ISBN 1-888974-08-7

Front cover painting: BIG HOG is a limited edition print by historical artist Jerry Crandall. It depicts a kill scored by Lt. Cdr. Tom Blackburn (BIG HOG) on November 11, 1943. His victim on that date was a JAAF Tony from the 68th Fighter Regiment based at Rabaul. Blackburn was the commanding officer of VF-17 which was based at Ondongo at that time. He finished the war with eleven confirmed victories, five probables, and three enemy aircraft damaged. Also seen in the painting is the Corsair flown by Blackburn's wingman, Doug Gutenkunst. The thoroughly researched print is copyrighted © 1988 by Jerry Crandall and Eagle Editions Ltd. Each numbered print in the limited edition is signed by Captain Tom Blackburn and the artist. For ordering information, contact Eagle Editions Ltd. P. O. Box 580, Hamilton, MT 59840.   (Print courtesy of Eagle Editions Ltd.)

Rear cover photo: Instrument panel details and colors in the National Museum of Naval Aviation's FG-1D are revealed in this large photograph. Additional pictures taken inside the cockpit of this Corsair can be found on page 37.

INTRODUCTION

A head-on view of the XF4U-1 prototype shows how the yellow paint on the top of the wings wrapped around the leading edge. The distinctive inverted gull wing design of the Corsair is best illustrated from this angle. (Vought)

Because of the unusual and distinctive design of its inverted gull wing, Vought's F4U Corsair became known as the "bent wing bird" to aviation enthusiasts. As it attacked the enemy on the ground, the air rushing through the radiators buried in its wing roots created a sound that the Japanese named "whistling death." But to the pilots who flew it, and to the Marines on the ground that it supported, the Corsair also became known as the "sweetheart of Okinawa." Regardless of what name it was called, the F4U Corsair was indisputably one of the most successful fighter designs in the history of military aviation.

At a time when advances in aircraft design were moving forward at an unprecedented rate, the Corsair remained in production for over a decade. It was designed as a fighter, but as evidence of the versatility of its outstanding design, it was also developed into an excellent fighter-bomber. Later a specialized ground attack variant, designated the AU-1, was produced. It became the first radar-equipped night fighter used by the Navy and Marines, and specialized photographic reconnaissance variants were also developed.

The success of the Corsair during World War II can be exemplified to a considerable extent simply by numerical data. In the air, it compiled an 11.3 to 1 kill to loss rate as its pilots shot down 2,140 enemy aircraft while losing only 189 Corsairs. This was the best ratio of any fighter in that war. F4Us flew over 64,000 sorties during World War II, making over 10,000 strikes against enemy airfields, 2,000 attacks on harbor areas, 2,800 raids against transportation facilities, and 4,000 attacks against ships of all types. They provided effective close air support to Marine and Army forces battling the Japanese on the ground. Five years after VJ Day, it again proved to be a valuable fighter-bomber and ground attack aircraft during the Korean War.

Although many publications have been written about the Corsair over the past fifty years, none have extensively discussed and illustrated the various changes and improvements made to the aircraft's design as a considerable number of variants and sub-variants were produced. In order to provide a comprehensive look at the Corsair's details and development from one version to another, two volumes in the Detail & Scale Series will be published. This book is part one, and it covers the XF4U-1 prototype, F4U-1, F4U-1A, F4U-1C, F4U-1D, F4U-2, XF4U-3, and F2G variants. Part two will include all production versions from the F4U-4 through the F4U-7. In this first part, most of the color pages will be dedicated to detailed photography, while in part two, the color section will have mostly general photographs of Corsairs.

In obtaining the detailed photographs for these two books, numerous Vought delivery photos were reproduced, and trips were made to photograph eleven different Corsairs which have been maintained in excellent condition over the years since they were retired from service. Among these were five different versions.

In both publications, each variant of the Corsair will be treated separately, and for each version that went into production, photographs and drawings will point out and illustrate the features, changes, and improvements that were made. The 1/72nd scale drawings in both books were created specifically for these two publications by Lloyd Jones who used the Vought factory blueprints and engineering drawings as references for their development.

Each of the two volumes on the Corsair concludes with our usual modelers section which provides reviews of the plastic model kits available for the versions of the F4U covered in that book.

DEVELOPMENTAL HISTORY

Only one prototype of the Corsair was built, and it was designated the XF4U-1. Its first flight took place on May 29, 1940, with Vought's Chief of Flight Tests, Lyman A. Bullard, Jr. at the controls. (Vought)

Note: The U. S. Navy continued to use the original F4U-1 designation for the Corsairs with the raised cockpit and the semi-bubble canopy for some time after these aircraft entered service. Later, in an effort to avoid confusion, an "A" suffix was added to the designation of these Corsairs, although the letter was not painted on the vertical tails of the aircraft. Early British Corsairs received the next letter suffix, thus becoming F4U-1Bs. The cannon armed variant was designated the F4U-1C, while the last production sub-variant in the "dash one" series was the F4U-1D. In this publication, these suffix letters will be used to distinguish one sub-variant from another. The use of the terms "F4U-1series" or "dash one series" will be used to refer to all sub-variants of the Corsair from the F4U-1 through the F4U-1D.

For the sake of simplicity, only the Vought designations will be used in most cases except when describing differences between aircraft built by Vought, Goodyear, and Brewster. For example, the use of the designation "F4U-1D," when making reference to features or providing information about that sub-variant, will also include the comparable FG-1D unless otherwise stated.

In the late 1930s, it appeared that the radial engine was on its way out as a powerplant for fighter aircraft. In fact, the U. S. Army Air Corps had asked Pratt & Whitney to stop development of radial engines completely and concentrate on inline liquid cooled designs. In the meantime, Allison was producing the V-1710 inline engine that was powering almost all of the USAAC fighters being produced or designed at that time. These included the Lockheed P-38 Lightning, Bell P-39 Airacobra, Curtiss P-40 Warhawk, and the early versions of the North American P-51 Mustang. Some versions of the P-40, and later variants of the P-51 would be powered by the Rolls Royce Merlin engine which was also a liquid cooled inline design. As far as the USAAC was concerned, the radial engine was not being considered for future fighter designs. They believed sleeker and more aerodynamic airframes, which could be fitted with inline engines, offered the best possibility of higher performance.

But the Navy recognized several advantages of the radial engine and believed that continued development was not only desirable, but it was absolutely necessary. Radials were simpler to maintain, and they were rugged and dependable. They could receive battle damage and keep on operating to bring both pilot and aircraft home. One bullet through the coolant tank in a liquid cooled powerplant meant that the engine would soon seize and cause the loss of the plane. These cooling systems were more complex and also required more maintenance.

The debate over the inline versus the radial engine was also taking place around the world. In England, the change was made almost entirely to the inline design, and every major British fighter during World War II had an inline engine. These included the Hurricane, Spitfire, Tempest, and Typhoon. The Germans realized the advantages of both designs, and while Messerschmitt used the inline powerplant in its Bf 109s, Focke Wulf chose radial engines for its Fw 190A. The majority of Japanese fighters were equipped with radial engines, but a few designs produced during the war had inline engines.

The Navy really did not have much use for inline powerplants, and they asked Pratt & Whitney to design the largest and most powerful radial engine ever developed for use in an aircraft up to that time. This request would result in the R-2800 Double Wasp that could produce 2,000 horsepower.

Meanwhile, the Navy had issued a design competition for a new shipboard fighter in February 1938. Vought proposed two similar designs called the V-166A and V-166B. The V-166A was to be powered by the existing Pratt & Whitney R-1830 Twin Wasp engine, while the V-166B was to be fitted with the new supercharged XR-2800-2 engine if the development of that powerplant continued successfully. To utilize the power

After its crash on July 11, 1940, the XF4U-1 was rebuilt, and on October 1, 1940, it became the first U. S. fighter to exceed 400 miles-per-hour in level flight. It is shown here as it appeared on April 19, 1941. (Vought)

produced by the R-2800, the largest propeller ever fitted to a fighter aircraft was designed by Hamilton-Standard. Its three blades had a diameter of thirteen feet, four inches.

To provide ground clearance for this huge propeller, while keeping the landing gear short and strong enough for carrier operations, Vought's design for the V-166B included a unique inverted gull wing. This feature also meant that the wing root could be joined to the fuselage at a ninety degree angle which was the most efficient design for both maximizing strength and minimizing drag. The inverted gull wing also improved visibility below the aircraft for the pilot, lowered the height of the folded wing, and made ditching at sea easier and safer.

The new fighter would also be the first to make extensive use of a new spot welding technique developed jointly by Vought and the Naval Aircraft Factory. This production process promised a very smooth skin which reduced drag and thus improved performance. The design was also the first to make use of the thrust from the engine exhausts to increase the speed.

The full scale mock-up was ready for inspection on February 8, 1939. After approval, Vought was authorized to build a single prototype designated the XF4U-1.

It took almost fifteen months of work at Vought's plant in Stratford, Connecticut, to complete the prototype. On May 29, 1940, Lyman A. Bullard Jr. lifted the aircraft off the runway at the Bridgeport Municipal Airport for an uneventful first flight which lasted thirty-eight minutes. But disaster struck on the fifth flight when Boone T. Guyton, running short on fuel, made a forced landing on the Norwich golf course. The plane flipped over on its back, crushing the tail section, and the right wing was completely torn off. But the ruggedness of the Corsair's design and construction paid off, because the XF4U-1 was repairable. This probably saved the development program for what would become one of America's most important fighters in World War II.

Over two months of intensive work were required to repair the prototype, but when it began flying again, it surpassed expected performance figures. On October 1, 1940, it became the first U. S. fighter to exceed 400 miles per hour in level flight. Such a feat could hardly go unnoticed by the U. S. Army Air Corps, and General "Hap" Arnold, having already been impressed by the XF4U-1s performance figures, began to look at Pratt & Whitney's big R-2800 as a possibility for use in a new Air Corps fighter.

While the XF4U-1 was being flight tested, Republic was working on a new design for a lightweight fighter powered by a liquid cooled inline engine. It was designated the XP-47A by the Army Air Corps, and by mid-1940, it had not progressed past the design phase. But because of the Navy's success with the R-2800 powerplant in the XF4U-1, the XP-47A design was completely discarded. The XP-47B which replaced it was a large fighter also powered by the R-2800. The XP-47B became the prototype for the famous P-47 Thunderbolt, the fighter that would eventually be produced in greater numbers than any other in U. S. history. (See Detail & Scale Volume 54.)

Flight testing did reveal a number of problems with the XF4U-1. Some were related to the engine, and Pratt & Whitney began working on solutions. There were problems with roll control, and numerous changes to the ailerons were tried. Some of these continued even after production of the F4U-1 began. In a landing attitude and at approach speeds, the port wing stalled before the right. This would continue to be one of the problems that prevented the Corsair's use aboard carriers in the U.S. Navy until it was finally solved.

On June 30, 1941, Vought was given a contract to build 584 F4U-1s. Another year passed before the first

The F4U-1 was the first production variant of the Corsair, and one is shown here on the assembly line on August 12, 1942. Note the type of national insignia used at that time as well as the stripes on the tips of the propeller blades. The red, yellow, and blue stripes were soon replaced with a yellow tip. (Vought)

F4U-1s move down the production line at Vought as they near completion and delivery to the Navy and Marines. (Vought)

production F4U-1, BuNo. 02153, made its initial flight on June 25, 1942. During that time, the design of the aircraft had undergone several significant modifications. Most noticeably, the cockpit had been moved thirty-two inches further aft. This was done so that a 237-gallon fuel tank could be located between the cockpit and the engine accessory compartment. With the addition of this fuselage tank, the two fuel tanks in the center wing section were deleted, but the two 63-gallon tanks in the outer wing panels were retained.

Some changes were made to make the Corsair easier to mass produce, while others were intended to increase the combat worthiness of the aircraft. These included the addition of armor around the cockpit and vital areas, self-sealing fuel tanks, and increased firepower. The prototype had two .30-caliber machine guns in the cowl and two .50-caliber guns in the wings. The cowl guns were deleted, and four more .50-caliber weapons were added to the wings, thus bringing the total to six. These were all located outside the arc of the propeller so that no synchronization would be needed. The prototype's provision for the anti-aircraft bombs was deleted, but the capability to carry a small Mark 14-2 bomb rack under each wing was added. Bombs up to 100 pounds in size could be loaded on these racks.

Minor changes in the production aircraft included a redesign of the tail gear, and the arresting hook was made an integral part of the tail gear assembly. The entire unit was covered by two doors when retracted. The framed canopy was redesigned, and it could be jettisoned in the event of an emergency. The XF4U-1's floatation bags were deleted from the wings, and the span of the ailerons was increased. The deflector plate flaps were changed to a NACA slotted design. The R-2800-4 engine used in the prototype was replaced with the R-2800-8 in production aircraft. It allowed the F4U-1 to reach 400 miles per hour at 20,000 feet and climb at 3,000 feet per minute. Its service ceiling was 37,200 feet.

As the likelihood of America's involvement in World War II increased, associate contractors were established for the production of several aircraft types. On November 1, 1941, Brewster Aeronautical Corporation was named the first associate contractor for the Corsair, and it would continue to produce the aircraft under the F3A-1 and F3A-1A designations through mid-1944. These corresponded to the Vought F4U-1 and F4U-1A respectively. But in July 1944, in spite of orders in a demanding wartime economy, poor management caused Brewster to go out of business. Only 735 Corsairs were built by Brewster before the company ceased production, and of these, 430 were delivered to the Royal Navy. The 305 received by the U. S. Navy and Marines were used in stateside training roles and were generally considered unfit for combat.

In December 1941, Goodyear was named the second associate contractor for the Corsair, and the versions it would build were designated FG-1, FG-1A, and FG-1D. These corresponded to the Vought F4U-1, F4U-1A, and F4U-1D respectively. In contrast to Brewster, during 1944 and 1945, Goodyear would actually produce more FG-1Ds than Vought built of the comparable F4U-1D. During World War II, Goodyear manufactured a total of 3,941 Corsairs including all three sub-variants.

Carrier qualifications for the F4U-1 began in September 1942 aboard the newly completed USS SANGAMON, CVE-26. A number of significant problems were noted immediately. The premature port wing stall, which first appeared on the prototype, could cause the aircraft to land hard on its left landing gear. Part of this problem was traced to the upwash from the huge propeller as it passed over the lowest part of the left wing. Repositioning the cockpit further aft decreased the already poor visibility over the aircraft's long nose, and the stiffness of the main landing gear resulted in a bounce upon landing that could cause the Corsair to miss the arresting cables and even skip over the wire barriers. These problems were also experienced later as VF-17 began to work up aboard the USS BUNKER HILL, CV-17. As a result, the Corsair was not considered ready for carrier operations,

An F4U-1 from VMF-213 is ready to launch from the USS COPAHEE, AVG-12, as the Marine squadron is delivered to Guadalcanal on March 29, 1943.   (USN via NMNA)

Major Greg J. Wiessenberger, the commanding officer of VMF-213, prepares to climb into the cockpit of his F4U-1 at Guadalcanal in June 1943.   (USN via NMNA)

and Vought continued to look for ways to eliminate the problems associated with carrier operations. Eventually, the problems would be solved or at least reduced to a point where the U. S. Navy was satisfied.

At NAS North Island, California, VF-12 was the first Corsair squadron to be formed. It was quickly followed by VF-17 at NAS Norfolk, Virginia. Originally assigned to the USS BUNKER HILL, CV-17, this squadron was reassigned to land operations after the Navy decided that the Corsair was not ready for carrier operations. VF-17 became the first Navy squadron to see combat with the Corsair, and it would later be called the greatest Navy fighter squadron of all time. In seventy-five days of combat, its pilots shot down 127 enemy aircraft while producing fifteen aces in the process.

On September 7, 1942, VMF-124 became the first Marine Corsair squadron when it was formed at Camp Kearney, California. It would become the first Corsair unit to see combat, and it flew its first action on February 12, 1943, at Guadalcanal. Lt. Kenneth Walsh of VMF-124 became the first Corsair ace and the first Corsair pilot to be awarded the Medal of Honor. He downed three Zeros on April 1, 1943, and three more on May 13.

The propeller is pulled through on this F4U-1 as the pilot sits in the cockpit prior to a mission on January 15, 1944. The aircraft was assigned to VMF-222 which was based on Vella La Vella. Note the original short tail gear, the framed canopy, and the lack of a spoiler on the leading edge of the right wing.   (USN via NMNA)

He would later finish the war with twenty-one victories.

When the Navy declared that the Corsair was not ready for carrier operations, it was a blessing for the Marines. While most Navy fighter squadrons received Grumman's excellent F6F Hellcat, a fighter which proved well suited for carrier operations, the Marines were given the Corsair. In the air, the Corsair was even better than the Hellcat, and it was certainly superior to the F4F Wildcat which existing Marine fighter squadrons had been flying. As these units re-equipped with the Corsair, and as new Marine fighter squadrons were formed, the Marines finally had a fighter that was superior to its Japanese adversaries, and they began to run up the score in aerial victories.

One remarkable story involves Lt. Alvin Jensen who was a pilot in "Pappy" Boyington's famous Black Sheep squadron, VMF-214. On August 28, 1943, Jensen got separated from his flight during a storm. He came out of the clouds right over a Japanese airfield, and he single-handedly began strafing aircraft on the ground. When he returned to his base, he claimed that he had destroyed twenty-four enemy aircraft. A photo reconnaissance mission the following day confirmed his extraordinary claim.

As F4U-1s, FG-1s, and F3A-1s began to enter service, modifications were made to some airframes so that additional roles could be performed. Several were modified to carry a K-21 aerial camera in the lower fuselage, and these were redesignated F4U-1Ps. More importantly, thirty-two F4U-1s were converted to F4U-2 night fighters, and they served with VF(N)-75, VF(N)-101, and VMF(N)-532 as the first radar equipped night fighters in service with the U. S. Navy and Marines. VMF(N)-532 later converted two more F4U-1s to F4U-2 standards, bringing the total number to thirty-four. Details of the F4U-2 night fighters are illustrated and discussed on pages 63 through 65.

The Royal Navy began receiving Corsairs in June 1943 at NAS Quonset Point, Rhode Island. Fleet Air Arm squadrons 1830 and 1831 were the first to acquire the new fighter, and by the end of the war, nineteen FAA squadrons would be equipped with the Corsair.

This initial delivery to the Royal Navy included ninety-five aircraft which the U. S. Navy designated F4U-1Bs. The British dropped the alpha-numeric designation and simply called these aircraft Corsair Is. They were the

Aircraft carriers in the Royal Navy had a lower overhead in the hangar bays than those in the U. S. Navy. Because of this, eight inches had to be removed from each wing tip, and this was done on all FAA Corsairs except for the Corsair I. This caused the tips of the wings to be blunt as seen in this photograph of a British Corsair III. (NMNA)

A total of thirteen Royal New Zealand Air Force squadrons flew Corsairs during and after the war. These F4U-1As are from No. 18 Squadron, and they are flying off the coast of Guadalcanal. (USN via NMNA)

only Corsairs to be delivered to the FAA without eight inches being clipped from each wing tip. The reduction in span was necessary to allow the Corsair to fit in the hangar bays of British carriers which had a lower overhead than U. S. ships.

The British also received 430 Brewster F3A-1s which they named the Corsair II. Vought F4U-1A and F4U-1Ds were called Corsair IIIs, while Goodyear FG-1s, FG-1As, and FG-1Ds were all called Corsair IVs. During World War II, 1,972 Corsairs of all types were delivered to the Royal Navy. Unlike the U. S. Navy, the Fleet Air Arm began operating their Corsairs from carriers right away, and with proper pilot training, they believed the aircraft could be used aboard ship with a reasonable degree of safety.

The first British use of the Corsair in Combat was on March 8, 1944. Squadrons 1834 and 1836 flew from HMS VICTORIOUS against the German Battleship TIRPITZ in Norway's Alten Fjord. Another strike against TIRPITZ was made on July 17, when Corsairs from HMS FORMIDABLE participated in the attack. But these would be the only actions where Corsairs would be used against the Germans. All other operations flown by Corsairs of the Royal Navy were carried out in the Pacific.

The only other nation to fly the Corsair during World War II was New Zealand. A total of 424 Corsairs were provided to the Royal New Zealand Air Force, and they were operated by thirteen squadrons. The first version to be supplied to the RNZAF was the F4U-1A, and 237 of this type were delivered. These were followed by 127 F4U-1Ds and 60 FG-1Ds.

Initial combat operations by Navy and Marine squadrons resulted in the usual requests for changes and improvements. The biggest problem concerned the forward visibility. To correct this, Vought raised the cockpit seven inches and covered it with a higher semi-bubble canopy which only had two frames at the top. The higher position of the pilot and the elimination of the side frames went a long way to improve visibility. These changes resulted in what would later become known as the F4U-1A. During production of this variant, the tail gear strut was lengthened to further improve visibility over the nose when the aircraft was on the ground or on a carrier deck.

The two small bomb racks that could be carried under the F4U-1's wings proved inadequate. VMF-111 and VF-17 fashioned "home made" racks in the field that could carry larger bombs on the centerline of the fuselage. Brewster then produced a similar but more substantial rack that could carry up to a 1000-pound bomb on the centerline station. Provisions for this rack were added to most F4U-1As during production. As an alternative, a 170-gallon external fuel tank could also be carried by these aircraft. During production of the F4U-1A, the R-2800-8 engine was replaced with the R-2800-8W which had water/alcohol injection to provide brief additional emergency power in combat situations. Additional information about the changes made to the F4U-1A can be found beginning on page 30.

The Corsair's capability as a fighter-bomber was further enhanced with the introduction of the F4U-1D. Two pylons were added under the center wing section. These could each carry a 1000-pound bomb, a napalm fire bomb, or a 154-gallon fuel tank. Even with these bombs or fuel tanks in place, a 170-gallon fuel tank could also be carried on the centerline. Most F4U-1Ds could

F4U-1As, beginning with BuNo. 50080, also had a tail gear strut that was lengthened by 6.48 inches to improve the pilot's visibility over the aircraft's long nose. These Corsairs are from VMF-224, and they were photographed on Majuro in August 1944. (USN via NMNA)

The F4U-1D/FG-1D was a true fighter-bomber variant of the Corsair, and it had two pylons under the center wing section to carry bombs, napalm, or fuel tanks. Four zero-length launchers were fitted under each wing for 5-inch rockets beginning with BuNo. 82253. This photograph was taken from a Marine Corps Avenger, and it shows escorting FG-1Ds from VMF-323 attacking Okinawa. FG-1Ds were the Goodyear equivalents of the Vought F4U-1Ds. *(USN via NMNA)*

FG-1Ds from VMF-512 share the flight deck with FM-2 Wildcats and TBM-3 Avengers aboard the USS SARGENT BAY, CVE-83. External fuel tanks are carried on the pylons under the center wing section of each of the Corsairs. *(USN via NMNA)*

also carry eight five-inch rockets under the outer wing panels on zero-length rocket stubs. During production of the F4U-1D, the canopy was further modified to eliminate the two overhead frames, and this resulted in what was known as the clear-vision canopy. Also during F4U-1D production, a change was made to a smaller propeller. The original Hamilton-Standard propeller, which had a diameter of 13' 4", was replaced by another similar Hamilton-Standard propeller with a diameter of only 13' 1". More information about the F4U-1D is provided starting on page 55.

After production of the F4U-1D began, small blocks of F4U-1Cs were alternated with the F4U-1Ds on the Vought production line. These had the same features as the F4U-1D, except that the six machine guns were replaced with four 20-mm cannon. Only 200 F4U-1Cs were produced, but they were the forerunner of several later cannon-armed Corsair variants. Additional information on the F4U-1C can be found on pages 52 through 54.

By the time the F4U-1D and F4U-1C entered production, Vought had solved the problems associated with carrier operations. The higher cockpit, frameless canopy, and heightened tail gear had combined to improve visibility as much as possible. A small spoiler had been added

On April 19, 1945, this F4U-1D from VMF-312 was the second aircraft to land at Kadena Air Field on Okinawa. It was flown by 1st Lt. Fred Borwell. *(USN via NMNA)*

to the right wing just outboard of the guns. This simple device caused the wings to stall at the same time, thus eliminating the port wing drop. The landing gear was modified to eliminate the bounce on landing. Trials aboard the USS GAMBIER BAY, CVE-73, proved that the Corsair was now ready for carrier operations in the U. S. Navy.

The F4U-1D was the first version to be deployed aboard carriers in considerable numbers, and the first carrier-based units were Marine squadrons VMF-124 and VMF-213 aboard the USS ESSEX, CV-9.

In early 1944, comparison testing with an F6F resulted in a finding by a Navy evaluation board that concluded the F4U was superior to the F6F as a fighter, and it was equal to the Hellcat as being suitable for carrier operations. Throughout the remainder of the war, Corsairs began to displace the F6F Hellcat in more and more Navy squadrons.

Other comparisons were flown against every other U. S. fighter and some captured enemy types. Below 13,000 feet, the Corsair was found to be an even match for the P-51 Mustang, and above that altitude the F4U was superior. Its overall superiority was demonstrated in tests with the P-38, P-39, P-40, and P-47 as well, and it proved to be an even match for the German Fw 190 in tests flown against a captured aircraft. It is foolish to claim that one type of aircraft was the best propeller-driven fighter of World War II, but the Corsair certainly deserved to be at or near the top of the list. Had it been used extensively in the European Theater, where access by the media would have been significantly greater than it was on remote island bases or aboard carriers, its excellence and exploits would have undoubtedly received more publicity.

The end of World War II did not mark the end of the Corsair. It would remain in production for almost seven more years, and it would prove to be a valuable weapon in Korea. As World War II came to a close, the F4U-4 was already in service and flying combat missions. The F4U Corsair in Detail & Scale, Part 2 begins with coverage of the F4U-4 and continues with all of the subsequent Corsair variants.

CORSAIR VARIANTS
XF4U-1 PROTOTYPE

The XF4U-1 prototype had a fuselage and tail section which were painted silver, while the top of each wing was chrome yellow. The national insignia was in all four wing positions.   *(Vought)*

The two similar photographs below were taken at two different times, and they illustrate an important change to the aircraft. The earlier photo at left shows the original propeller fitted to the prototype, and it was taken prior to the crash that caused considerable damage to the aircraft. At right, the XF4U-1 is shown as it appeared in April 1941 after it had been rebuilt. The propeller has been changed to one with broader blades and a more rounded tip. Stalling problems with the left wing were traced to the large propeller, and it took considerable time before this was corrected to the point where the Navy considered the Corsair safe enough for use on aircraft carriers.
(Both Vought)

Although the basic lines that would remain with the Corsair through all production variants were unmistakable on the one XF4U-1 prototype, it was a unique aircraft with features not found on any other F4U version.

The cockpit was almost three feet further forward in the fuselage, and the entire 273 gallons of internal fuel was carried in four tanks in the wings. Two were in the center wing section, while the other pair was located near the leading edge of the outer wing panels. Also located in the wings were flotation bags that could be deployed in the event of a ditching at sea. The XR-2800-2 engine was originally planned for the XF4U-1, but this was replaced with an XR-2800-4.

A framed canopy was installed, but it was considerably different in design than the one which would be used later on production F4U-1s. The windscreen had a telescopic sight fitted initially, but this was later deleted.

Armament consisted of two .30-caliber machine guns

The XF4U-1 had an oval shaped window in the lower fuselage. Early production Corsairs also had a window in this location, but it was rectangular in shape. Other underside details of the prototype are also visible in this flying view. (Vought)

mounted in the cowling with 750 rounds of ammunition for each weapon. A single .50-caliber gun was mounted in each wing, and 300 rounds were provided for each of these guns. Designers also intended for the Corsair to use small 5.2-pound anti-aircraft bombs as part of its armament, and this feature was included on the prototype. In utilizing these weapons, the pilot would fly the fighter above an enemy bomber formation and drop the anti-aircraft fragmentation bombs into it. A total of forty bombs could be carried with four bombs being loaded into each of ten compartments in the outer wing sections. A teardrop shaped bomb aiming window was located in the lower fuselage beneath the cockpit so that the pilot could line up his targets before releasing the bombs. This feature necessitated the floorless cockpit that would remain standard through the production of the F4U-1D.

A front view with the wings folded provides a good look at the propeller, cowling, and engine details of the prototype. (Vought)

After crashing during its fifth test flight, the prototype was rebuilt and fitted with a propeller of slightly different design. It had an empty weight of 7,418 pounds and a gross weight of 9,375 pounds. Rate of climb was 2,600 feet per minute, and the service ceiling was 35,500 feet. On October 1, 1940, it made history when it became the first U. S. fighter to exceed 400 miles per hour in level flight, and its maximum speed was rated at 405 miles per hour. Range was 1,070 statute miles. In almost every case, these performance figures were in excess of what was expected.

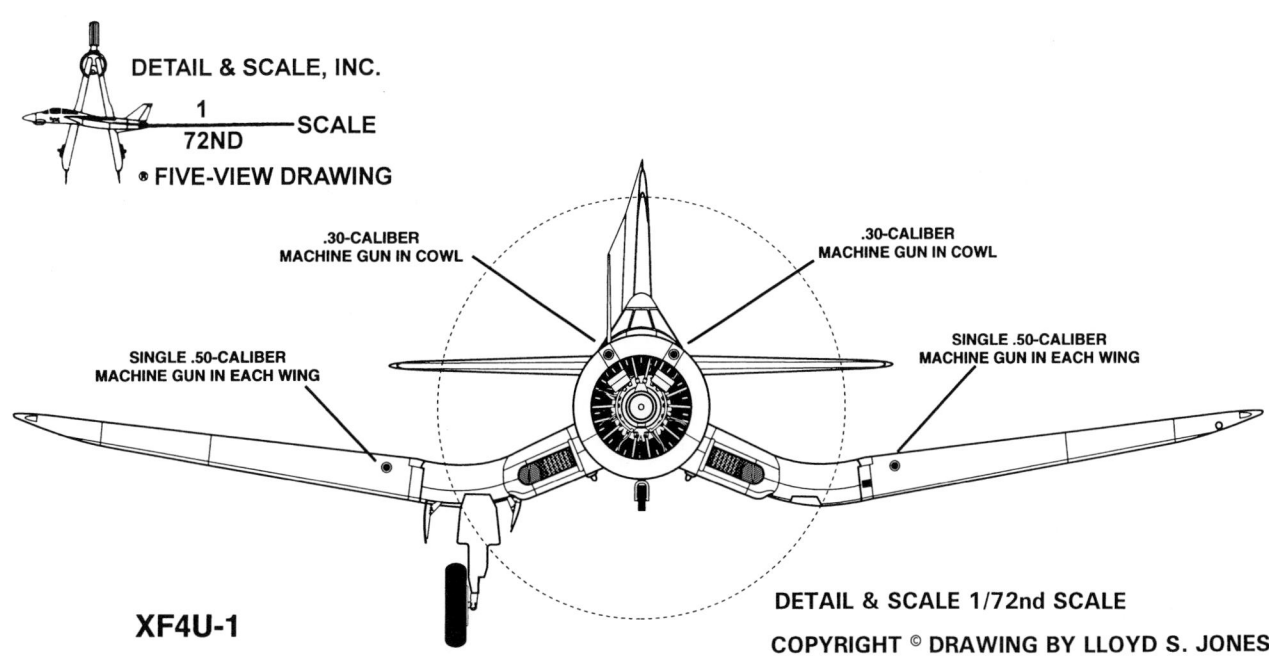

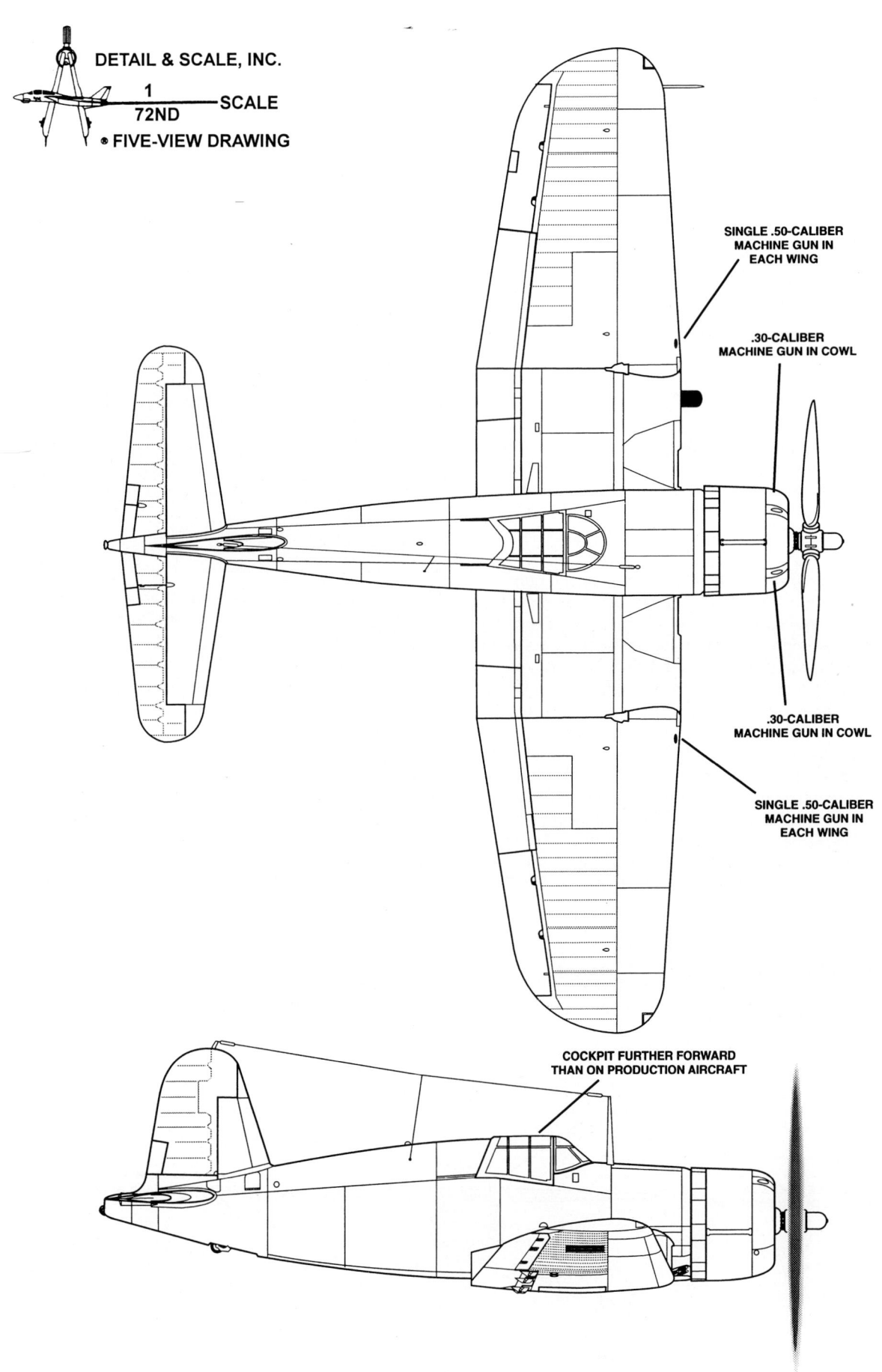

DETAIL & SCALE 1/72nd SCALE COPYRIGHT © DRAWINGS BY LLOYD S. JONES

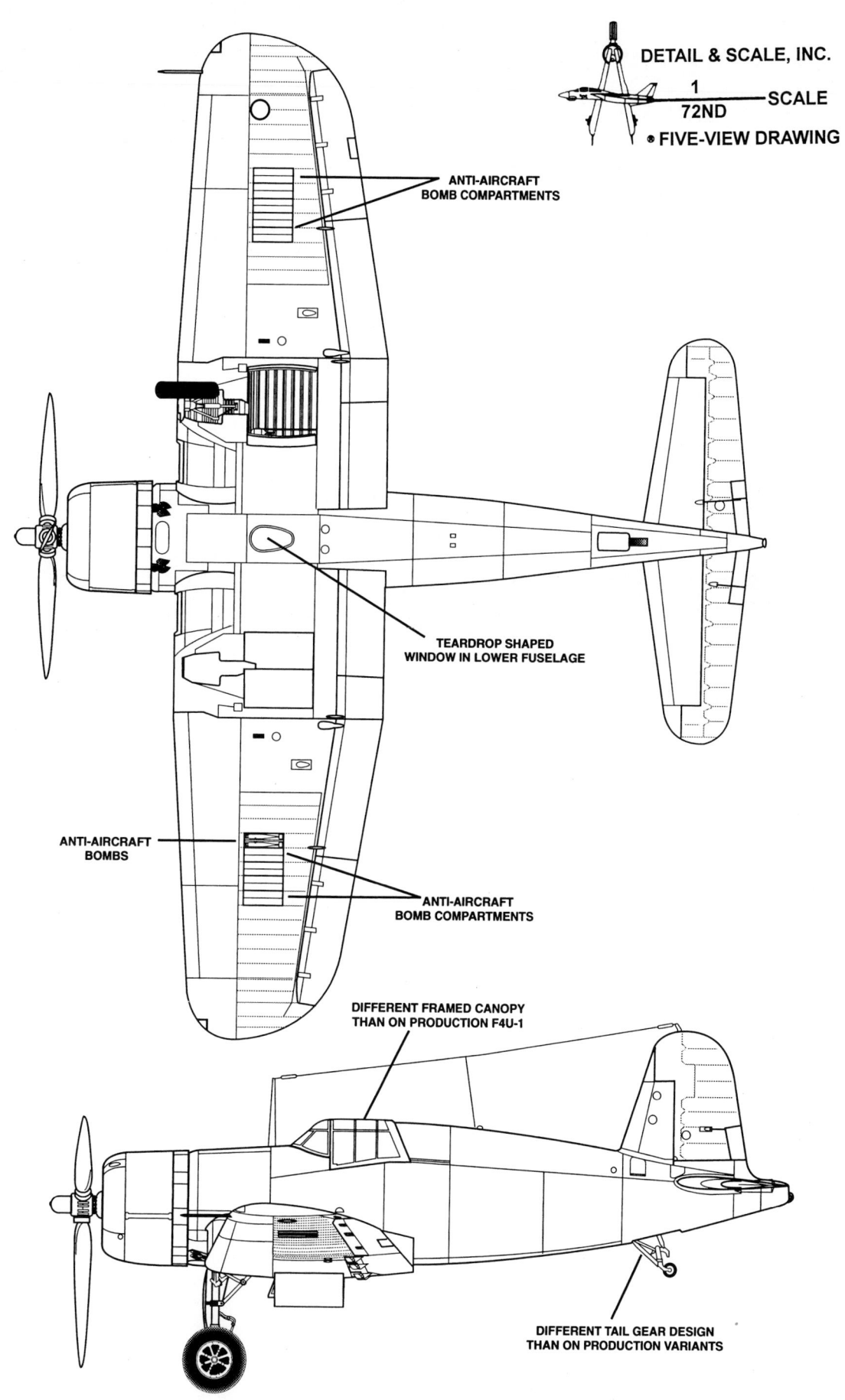

DETAIL & SCALE 1/72nd SCALE COPYRIGHT © DRAWINGS BY LLOYD S. JONES

XF4U-1 DETAILS

COCKPIT DETAILS

Details of the instrument panel in the XF4U-1 are visible here. No gun sight or eyebrow armament panels were installed. (Vought)

The seat had lap belts but no shoulder harnesses. Like the production F4U-1 through F4U-1D, there was no floor in the cockpit. Instead, there were two foot troughs below the rudder pedals. (Vought)

Details on the left side of the cockpit are illustrated in this photograph. The throttle quadrant, trim wheels, and fuel selector switch are all visible. A document and map case is on the side of the console. (Vought)

Here is a look at the right side of the cockpit in the prototype. All of the photographs on this page were taken on April 3, 1941, well after the aircraft had been rebuilt following its crash. (Vought)

The rear bulkhead in the cockpit had a tube at the top which could be used to house a life raft. It is shown here with the cover removed. (Vought)

The cover for the tube had the headrest on the outside as shown here. (Vought)

The lack of a floor in the cockpit is clearly evident here, and with the seat removed, additional details in the bottom of the fuselage are visible. The bomb aiming window is also evident. The tube under and forward of the control column provides cockpit cooling air. (Vought)

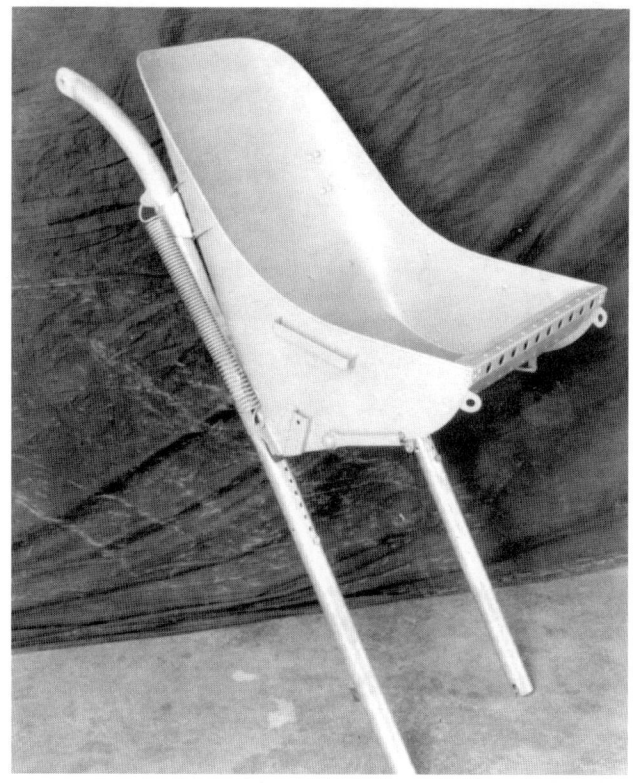

Details of the seat used in the XF4U-1 can be seen here. It was adjustable in height as indicated by the holes in the supporting legs and the tension spring. (Vought)

ENGINE DETAILS

Details of the cowling and cowl flaps are illustrated here. Note the openings for the right cowl machine gun in the upper cowl ring. (Vought)

Taken on February 2, 1940, this photograph shows the powerplant section of the XF4U-1 during construction. Note how air taken in through the intakes in the wing roots was routed into the ducting on the side of the engine compartment. (Vought)

Additional details are shown in this left side view. The XR-2800-2 powerplant was quickly replaced with an XR-2800-4 in the XF4U-1 prototype, but the appearance of the XR-2800-4 was practically identical to the XR-2800-2 illustrated in the photographs on this page. As Pratt & Whitney continued to make improvements to the engine, the XR-2800-4 gave way to the R-2800-8 by the time the first F4U-1s rolled off the production lines. (Vought)

The XF4U-1 prototype was initially powered by a Pratt & Whitney XR-2800-2 engine. The design of the crank case and the forward row of cylinders is visible in this right front view. (Vought)

Here is a look at the rear of the XR-2800-2 as seen from the right side. (Vought)

LANDING GEAR DETAILS

The basic design of the short, strong, main landing gear used on the prototype changed very little throughout the production of all Corsair variants. Only relatively small detail changes were made. The design of the original main gear wheel is also shown here. (Vought)

The right main gear is shown again from the inside. Note the oleo, scissors link, and hydraulic lines running down to the inside of the wheel. (Vought)

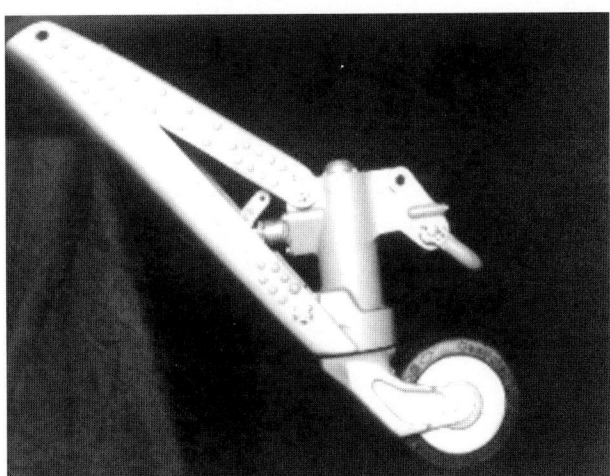

The tail gear used on the prototype was quite different than what was used on production aircraft. It was simple in design and very short in height. A solid rubber tire was fitted. (Vought)

Right: The interior of the tail wheel well is shown here. Note the hydraulic strut between the tail wheel assembly and the framework inside the well. (Vought)

WING DETAILS

Much of the skin on the outer wing panels were covered by fabric. With the fabric not yet installed, the framework of the wing is visible. The ailerons were also covered with fabric, but the flaps were skinned with sheet metal. *(Vought)*

Designers originally intended for the Corsair to carry small fragmentation bombs that could be dropped into formations of enemy bombers, and this feature was installed on the prototype. This view looks up into the bomb compartment under the right wing, and two of the small bombs can be seen in place. This feature was not installed on production Corsairs. *(Vought)*

The prototype had a .50-caliber machine gun installed in each wing, and the ammunition box was located just outboard of the weapon. This is the machine gun in the left wing. *(Vought)*

The right wing machine gun is visible here as is the line indicating the location of the wing fold. Note the open panel over the main hinge. This panel could be found on all production Corsairs as well. *(Vought)*

Because of the inverted gull wing design and the fact that the wings folded, the flaps had to be divided into three sections on each wing. These are the flaps on the right wing as seen during construction of the prototype. *(Vought)*

A spanner was used to fill the gap between the inner and center flaps on each wing when the flaps were lowered. This filled in the gap between the two flaps caused by the inverted gull design of the wing. It would remain a feature of all Corsair variants. *(Vought)*

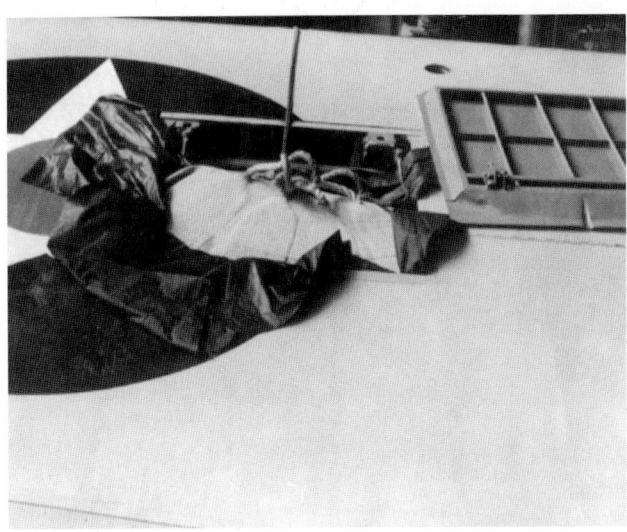

The XF4U-1 also had air bags that were installed in compartments in the top of the wings. They were designed to inflate to help the aircraft remain afloat in the event of a ditching at sea. The compartment in the left wing is shown here, and the uninflated air bag is partially pulled out on the wing. (Vought)

This view from behind the prototype shows the two air bags inflated as they would have been in an emergency ditching. In an effort to save weight, this feature was not installed on any production version of the Corsair. Even without these bags, Corsairs usually stayed afloat long enough for the pilot to get out of the cockpit when a ditching at sea was necessary. (Vought)

Above and below: Details of the wing fold on the prototype are revealed in these two views. Also note the outer flaps in the raised position. Compare these two photographs with those on page 45 that show the wing fold details on an FG-1D. (Both Vought)

The outer flap on the right wing is shown here from the underside. (Vought)

FUSELAGE DETAILS

Above: The canopy on the prototype was framed, but it was considerably different from what would later be installed on the production F4U-1. The trailing edge was angled, and the canopy tapered in height from front to rear along the rails. (Vought)

Left: A camera could be installed on a mount on the right side of the fuselage just below the windscreen. (Vought)

The cooling flap for the engine accessory compartment was located under the fuselage. This same design was used on all production variants of the Corsair through the F4U-1D, but it was changed beginning with the F4U-4 when a larger flap was installed. (Vought)

The arresting hook on the XF4U-1 was not part of the tail wheel assembly as it was on production aircraft. Instead, it slid into the rear of the fuselage like those on Hellcats as well as most Avengers and Helldivers. (Vought)

F4U-1

The F4U-1 was the first production version of the Corsair. It was considerably different from the prototype, and it was the only production variant with a birdcage or framed canopy. Early F4U-1s had a framed canopy with a flat top and a periscope as shown here, but later canopies had a blister on top for a rear-view mirror. Also note the glass in the rear window on this early aircraft. (Vought)

The first production F4U-1, BuNo. 02153, made its initial flight on June 25, 1942. It, and the production F4U-1s that followed, had several significant design changes when compared to the XF4U-1 prototype.

The two fuel tanks in the center wing section were deleted in favor of a 237-gallon tank in the fuselage. Locating this large tank directly behind the engine accessory compartment meant that the cockpit had to be moved aft thirty-two inches. The two 63-gallon tanks in the outer wing sections remained as they were on the prototype. F4U-1s had no provision for carrying any fuel in external tanks. Up front, the R-2800-8 engine replaced the XR-2800-4 used on the prototype.

The windscreen and canopy were redesigned, although the new jettisonable canopy was still a framed type that restricted visibility. Early canopies were flat on top and fitted with a Brownscope periscope, but this was later replaced with a rear view mirror located inside a blister at the forward top end of the canopy.

The firepower was significantly increased over what was installed in the prototype. Originally, the plan was simply to add a second .50-caliber machine gun to each wing so that the armament would include four .50-caliber guns in the wings and the two .30-caliber machine guns in the cowling. But it was decided to use weapons of the same caliber, so the cowl guns were deleted, and three .50-caliber machine guns were installed in each wing. Each inboard and center gun had 400 rounds of ammunition, and each outboard gun was provided with 375 rounds. The provision for anti-aircraft bombs was deleted, but a Mark 14-2 bomb rack could be fitted under each wing. Each rack could carry a 100-pound bomb.

Other changes were made to the wings. The floatation bags were deleted from each wing to save weight. The aileron span was increased to improve roll rate, and a balance tab was added to the inboard end of each aileron during production of the F4U-1. The deflector plate flaps used on the prototype were replaced with NACA slotted flaps.

Some changes improved the survivability of the aircraft in combat. Armor was added around the cockpit to protect the pilot, and bulletproof glass was located under the windscreen. The fuel tanks were changed to the self-sealing type.

The tail landing gear was completely redesigned. The arresting hook, which had been a separate assembly

F4U-1s had a window in the lower fuselage, but it was rectangular in shape rather than being oval shaped like the one on the prototype. This window was on some early F4U-1As as well, but it was deleted during production of that variant. The windows were painted over on some aircraft, and they were not considered useful. (Vought)

21

F4U-1s of VMF-222 are readied for a mission from Vella La Vella in August 1943. (NMNA)

on the prototype, was made part of the tail landing gear structure, and when retracted, the tail gear/arresting hook combination fit into a well that was covered by two doors. A slot was at the center of the doors that allowed the tire to protrude slightly.

Almost all F4U-1s, F3A-1s, and FG-1s were delivered in the two-tone paint scheme of non-specular Blue Gray on the upper and vertical surfaces and non-specular Light Gray on the bottom surfaces. A very few of these aircraft at the end of the production run were delivered in the tri-color paint scheme of Sea Blue, Intermediate Blue, and white. All three of these colors were non-specular.

Comparable FG-1s were built by Goodyear, while Brewster produced the F3A-1. F4U-1s delivered to Britain were originally designated F4U-1Bs by the U. S. Navy. The British called their Vought F4U-1s Corsair Is, and these were the only Fleet Air Arm Corsairs not to have eight inches clipped from each wing. F3A-1s in the Royal Navy were known as Corsair IIs, while FG-1s (and FG-1Ds) were designated Corsair IVs.

A Fleet Air Arm Corsair I is shown in flight with standard British markings. Corsair Is did not have the eight inches clipped from each wing tip, but all subsequent FAA Corsairs did to provide clearance in the hangar bays of British aircraft carriers. Many FAA Corsairs were painted in a gray and green camouflage. Also note that the turtledeck windows have been completely deleted from this aircraft. (Vought)

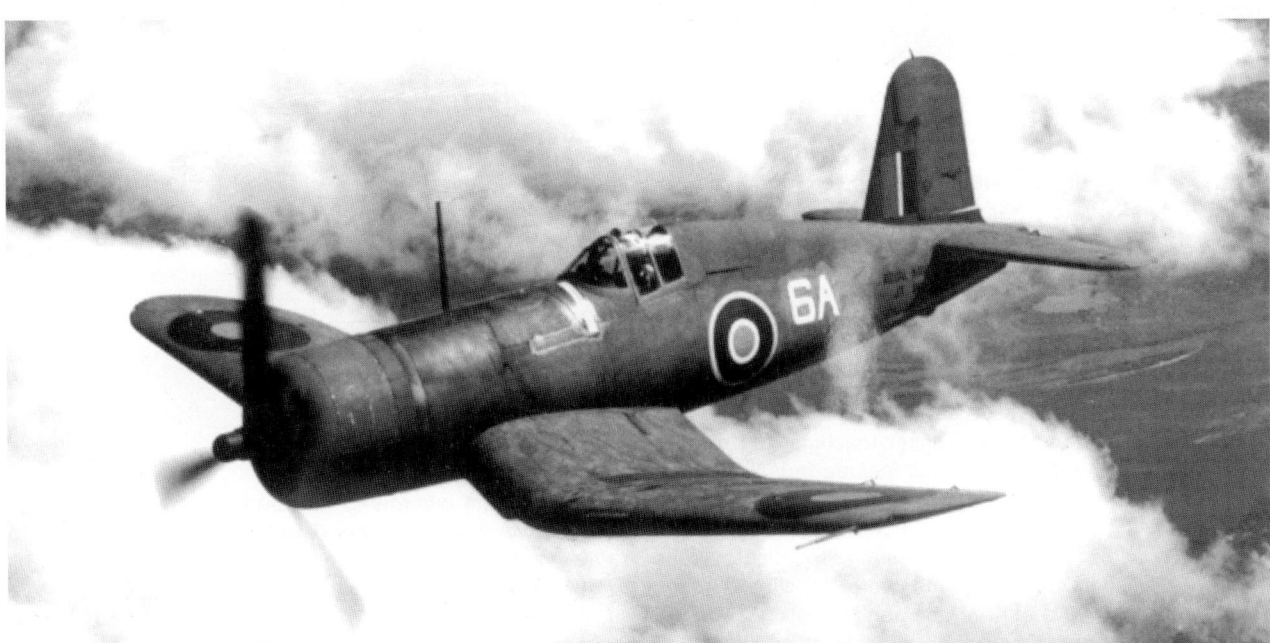

F4U-1 DETAILS

Radio masts on the F4U-1 and other production versions of the Corsair varied depending on the radio equipment carried. One was often fitted on the spine as shown here, while a second could be mounted on the forward fuselage. But some aircraft had neither. This F4U-1 has an antenna wire that enters the fuselage just to the right of the mast and a little forward of it, but as with the masts, the antenna wire arrangement varied. (Vought)

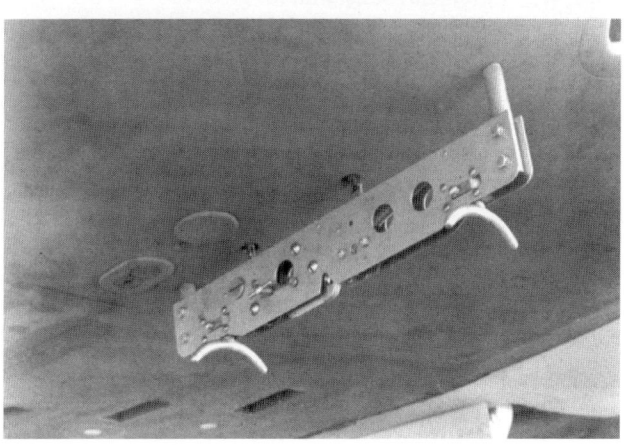

Bombs in the 100-pound class could be carried on bomb racks that were fitted under the outer wing panels on the F4U-1. This was seldom, if ever, used operationally in combat. (Vought)

Details of the right wing fold on an F4U-1 are illustrated in this photo. (Vought)

Details on the underside of the left wing of an F4U-1 are shown here. Note that the trim tab is present on the left aileron, but there is no balance tab at the inboard end of the aileron. A balance tab was added to each aileron during production of the F4U-1, and it remained standard on subsequent versions. It is interesting to note that the ailerons were made of plywood and covered with fabric. The shell ejection slots for the three left machine guns are visible in this photograph as is the retractable landing/taxi light near the tip. This light was only on F4U-1s and early production F4U-1As. It was replaced with an approach light in the leading edge of the left wing during F4U-1A production starting with BuNo. 17930. (Vought)

The tail section on the F4U-1 would remain unchanged until the production of the F4U-5. Two tabs were located on each elevator, with the inboard one in each case being a standard trim tab and the outer one being a balance tab. The large rudder had a single trim tab which had its actuator on the left side. Both the rudder and elevators were fabric covered. (Vought)

23

COCKPIT DETAILS

Left and above: Details of the F4U-1's cockpit are revealed in these two photographs that were taken during production of the aircraft. (Vought)

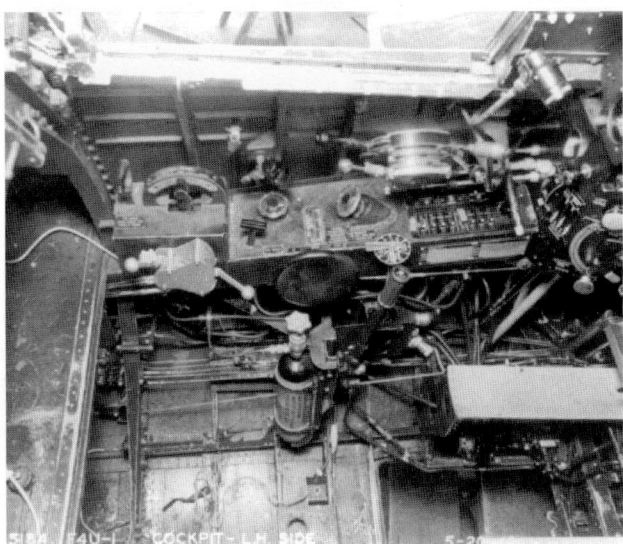

With the seat not yet installed, features on the left side of the cockpit are clearly visible. The arrangement of items inside the cockpit was relatively haphazard when compared to the F4U-4 and later variants. (Vought)

Like the prototype, the F4U-1 did not have a cockpit floor. Instead, there were foot troughs just below the rudder pedals. Anything dropped inside the cockpit could become hopelessly lost in the lower fuselage. (Vought)

ENGINE DETAILS

Above: The F4U-1 was powered by the R-2800-8 or -8W engine. This is the right side of a powerplant section that is ready for installation on the aircraft. (Vought)

Right: Easy access to the cylinder heads could be gained by removing several panels all the way around the cowling. (Vought)

Cooling flaps completely encircled the cowling on the F4U-1. They are seen here in the open position. The flaps at the top were later sealed closed to help prevent oil from blowing past them and on to the windscreen. (Vought)

.50-CALIBER MACHINE GUN ARMAMENT

Standard internal armament for the F4U-1 and most other production Corsairs was six .50-caliber machine guns located in the wings. This is an overall view of the gun installation in the left wing. (Vought)

This close-up provides a better look at the three left guns and their ammunition chutes. Chromate Yellow primer was applied to the interior of the gun bays. (Vought)

The ammunition boxes were installed outboard of the guns on each wing. These are the ammunition boxes in the left wing. (Vought)

The right gun bay is shown here, and the inboard gun has been removed. (Vought)

Details of the framed canopy as used on the F4U-1 are visible here. Although the top two pieces of glass have been removed, the design of the framework is apparent. Note that the aft piece of glazing on each side does not have any framework along its rear edge. (Webster)

During F4U-1 production, the framed canopy was modified so that it had a blister at the top for a rear view mirror. This blister, as well as the mirror inside of it, is clearly visible here. Also note that the recessed area for the fixed rear window has been covered over on this aircraft. (Vought)

The tail wheel on the F4U-1 was fully retractable, but the strut was short. The arresting hook was attached to the framework of the gear. This assemby has the hard rubber tire used primarily for carrier operations. (Vought)

When the landing gear was retracted, the tire did not fit fully inside of the doors. Instead, it partially protruded through a slot in the doors. In this case, a pneumatic tire is fitted on the tail wheel. (Vought)

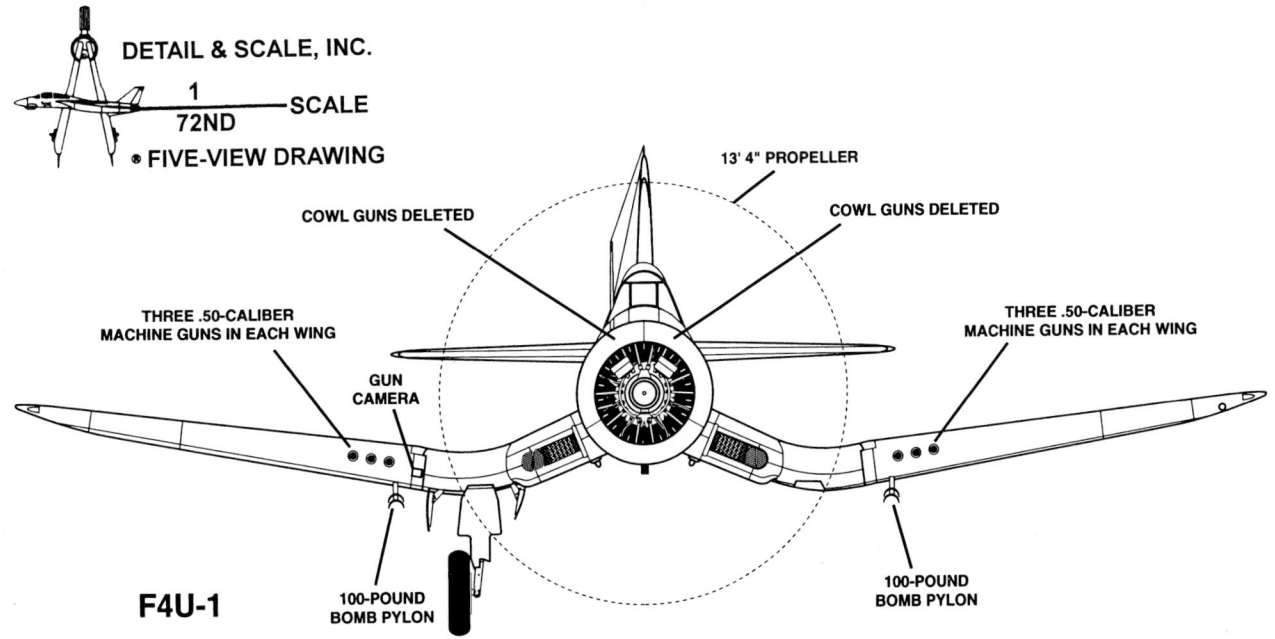

DETAIL & SCALE 1/72nd SCALE COPYRIGHT © DRAWING BY LLOYD S. JONES

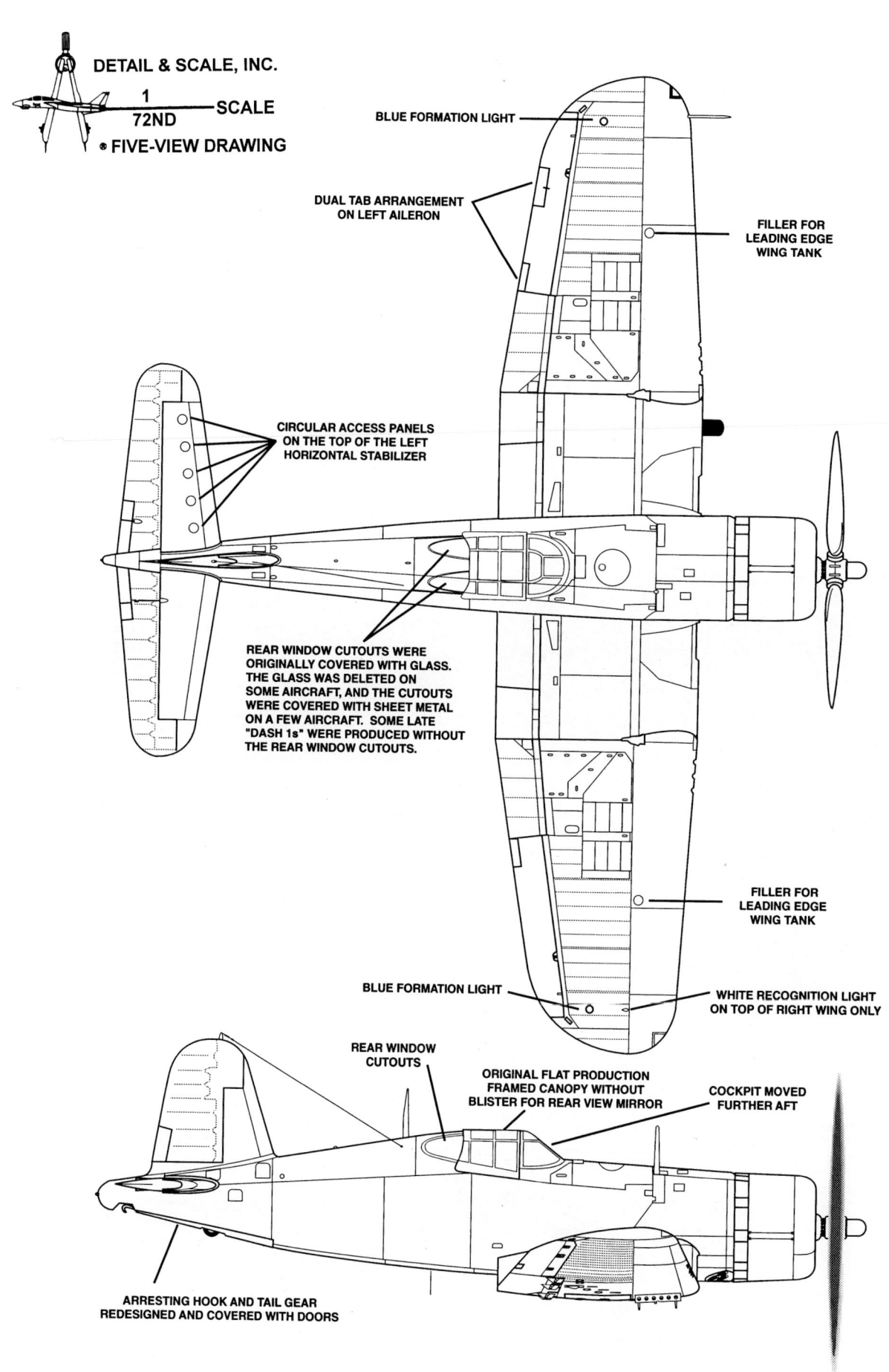

DETAIL & SCALE 1/72nd SCALE COPYRIGHT © DRAWINGS BY LLOYD S. JONES

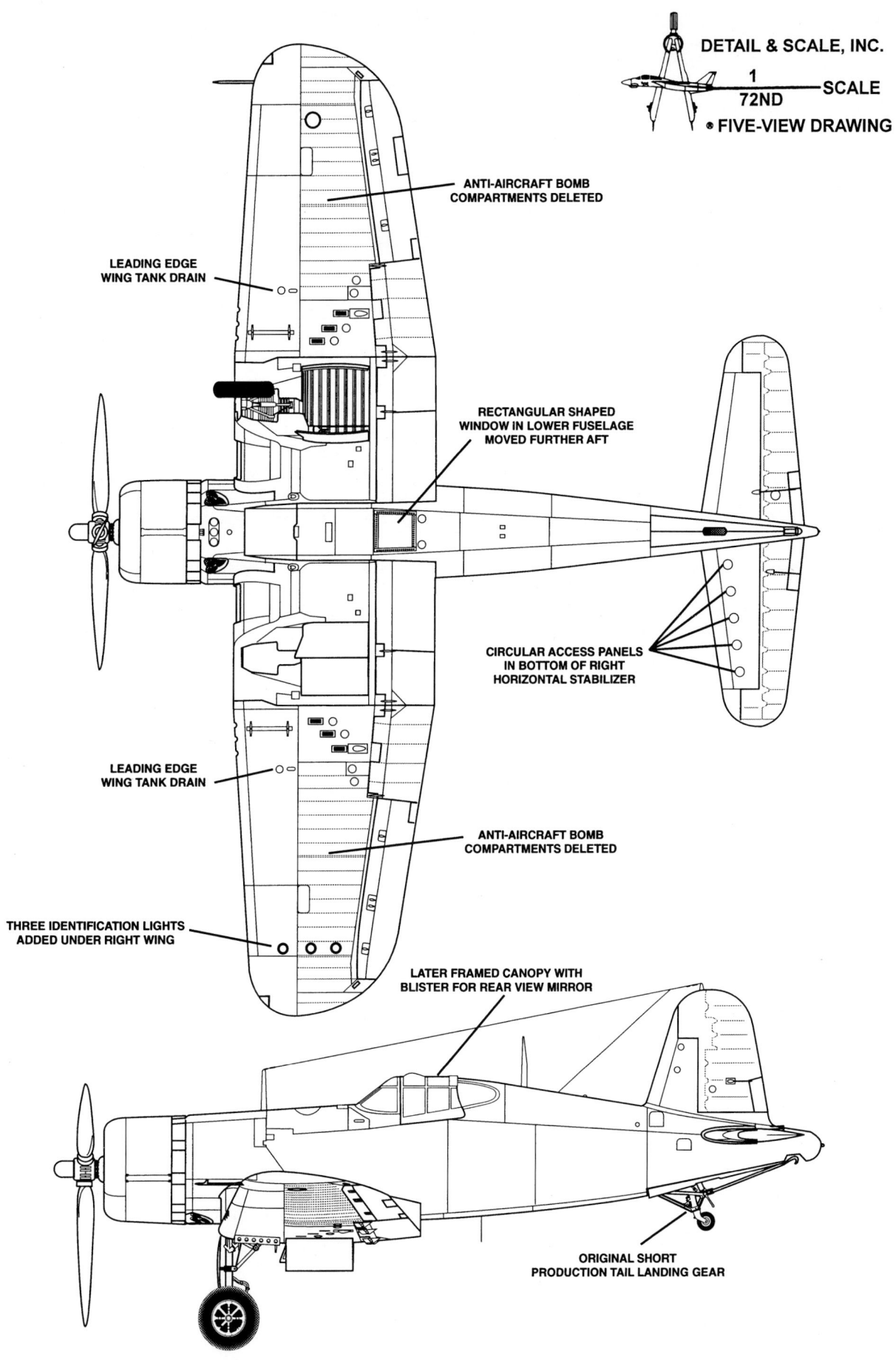

DETAIL & SCALE 1/72nd SCALE COPYRIGHT © DRAWINGS BY LLOYD S. JONES

F4U-1A

Two features which were introduced on the F4U-1A were both intended to improve visibility. These included the semi-bubble canopy and the taller tail wheel strut, both of which are visible on this factory fresh aircraft. The taller tail wheel assembly, which was lengthened 6.48 inches, was added during production with BuNo. 50080. Late in the production of the F4U-1, the paint scheme had been changed to the three-tone camouflage of Sea Blue, Intermediate Blue, and flat white, and this continued to be used on the F4U-1A. *(Vought)*

Although the "A" suffix was not added to the designation painted on the vertical tail of these aircraft, official documentation and manuals subsequently referred to the first Corsairs that had raised cockpits and a redesigned canopy and windscreen with the F4U-1A designation.

For the most part, changes that differentiated the F4U-1A from the previous F4U-1 were made to improve pilot visibility. The cockpit was raised seven inches, and the vertical travel for the seat was increased. The framed canopy was replaced with a higher semi-bubble design that had only two lateral frames at the top. The higher position of the pilot, along with the elimination of the side frames, significantly improved visibility in all directions except forward. The Corsair's long nose still restricted the forward line of sight, particularly in a nose high landing attitude. In a further effort to reduce the severity of this problem, the tail wheel strut was lengthened 6.48 inches beginning with F4U-1A, BuNo. 50080.

As designed, the Corsair had two bomb racks which could only carry small bombs in the 100-pound class. In an effort to increase the bomb-carrying capability of their aircraft, some units in the field created a centerline rack that could carry a bomb up to the 1000-pound size. A

This F4U-1A was photographed in August 1944 aboard the USS KWAJALEIN, CVE-98. It was assigned to VMF-321 and flown by Lt. J. T. O'Connell. Note the three identification lights under the right wing tip. Tape protects the shell ejector slots under the wing. *(USN via NMNA)*

The F4U-1A was the first version of the Corsair which could be fitted with an external fuel tank. Provisions to carry a 170-gallon tank on the centerline station were added beginning with BuNo. 13572. *(Vought)*

Brewster built F3A-1As which were comparable to the Vought F4U-1A. This one was assigned to a training unit in January 1946. Although the -1As were delivered in the tri-color paint scheme, most that remained in service after mid-1945 were repainted in the overall gloss Sea Blue scheme as shown here. *(USN via NMNA)*

more substantial rack of similar design was developed and produced by Brewster, and the capability to utilize this rack was added on F4U-1A, BuNo. 17930, and FG-1, BuNo. 13572. At the same time, provisions were also installed to permit the use of a dropable 170-gallon fuel tank on the centerline station. Either this tank or the bomb rack could be carried, but both could not be used simultaneously. Records do not indicate when this provision was installed on F3A-1As, but as evidenced by the photograph above, these Brewster Corsairs could also be fitted with the centerline bomb rack.

Another change that began with F4U-1A, BuNo. 17930, was the elimination of the retractable landing/taxi light under the left wing. It was replaced with a smaller approach light located in the leading edge of the wing. This same change was first incorporated on FG-1A, BuNo. 13261, and F3A-1A, BuNo. 04592.

Water/alcohol injection first appeared in the form of the R-2800-8W engine on F4U-1A, BuNo. 55910, FG-1A, BuNo. 13992, and F3A-1A, BuNo. 11208. This feature could be used for a few minutes to provide emergency power in a combat situation.

As efforts continued to solve the problems with the premature stalling of the left wing, a small spoiler was added to the leading edge of the right wing just outboard of the guns. This small spoiler was only six inches long, but it was enough to cause the right wing to stall at the same time as the left, thus keeping the aircraft level.

All F4U-1As, F3A-1As, and FG-1As that were delivered to the U. S. Navy and Marines were painted in the tri-color paint scheme of non-specular Sea Blue on the upper surfaces, non-specular Intermediate Blue on the vertical surfaces, and flat white on the bottom surfaces. It should be noted that the bottoms of the outer wing panels were painted Intermediate Blue, since they were considered a vertical surface when the wings were folded. Exposure to the sun and repainting in the field often left all of the upper and vertical surfaces a faded medium blue with no distinction between the Sea Blue and Intermediate Blue colors.

An F4U-1A is about to be launched from an escort carrier. Most of the Corsair's problems with carrier operations were related to making an arrested recovery. Even before the U. S. Navy considered them safe for full carrier operations, Corsairs were routinely delivered to land bases by escort carriers. A crane loaded the aircraft aboard the ship from a pier, and when they were close enough to their destination, they were launched by catapult or simply flown off in a deck run. *(USN via NMNA)*

F4U-1A DETAILS

Above: This close-up shows the new semi-bubble canopy as used on F4U-1As and early F4U-1Ds. (Vought)

Right: A top view shows the two frames running laterally across the canopy. These were on all canopies used on F4U-1As. During the production run of F4U-1Ds, these frames were deleted beginning with BuNo 57583, and their elimination provided even better visibility. (Vought)

The original design for the taller tail gear assembly is shown here. Compare this to the production design illustrated on page 62. Also note how the Intermediate Blue is sprayed over the white under the horizontal tail. The tail gear was usually painted light gray or a steel color. (Vought)

The interior of the tail wheel well as used on the F4U-1A is shown here. The doors retained the cutouts to allow the tire to remain partially exposed when the gear was retracted. The interior of the doors was usually the same color as the underside of the fuselage. The interior of the wheel well was often the same color, but it was sometimes Chromate Yellow Primer or an unusual salmon brown color.

Coverage of the F4U-1A continues on page 49.

COLOR GALLERY
CORSAIR PAINT SCHEMES

XF4U-1 PROTOTYPE MAY 1940

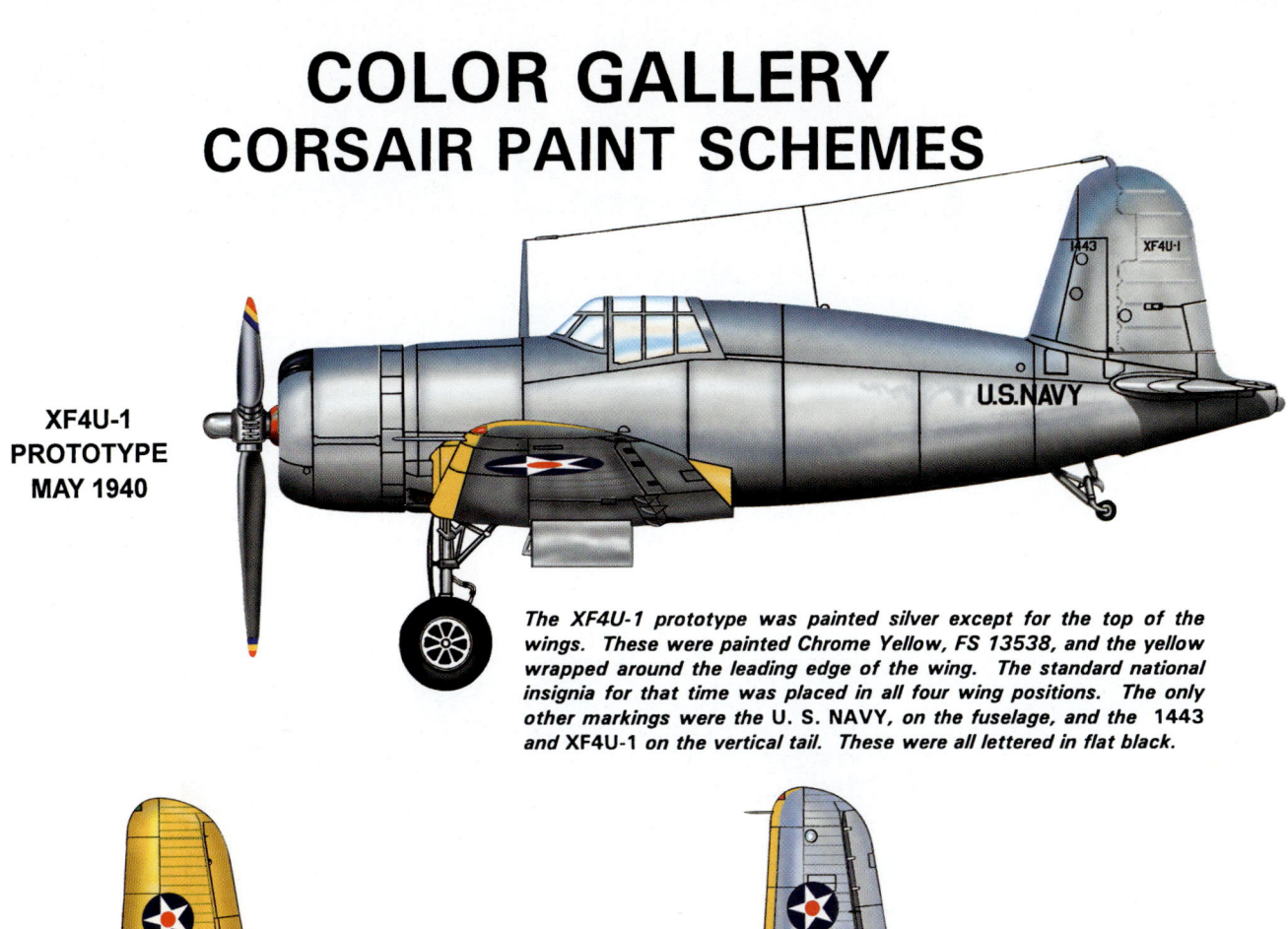

The XF4U-1 prototype was painted silver except for the top of the wings. These were painted Chrome Yellow, FS 13538, and the yellow wrapped around the leading edge of the wing. The standard national insignia for that time was placed in all four wing positions. The only other markings were the U. S. NAVY, on the fuselage, and the 1443 and XF4U-1 on the vertical tail. These were all lettered in flat black.

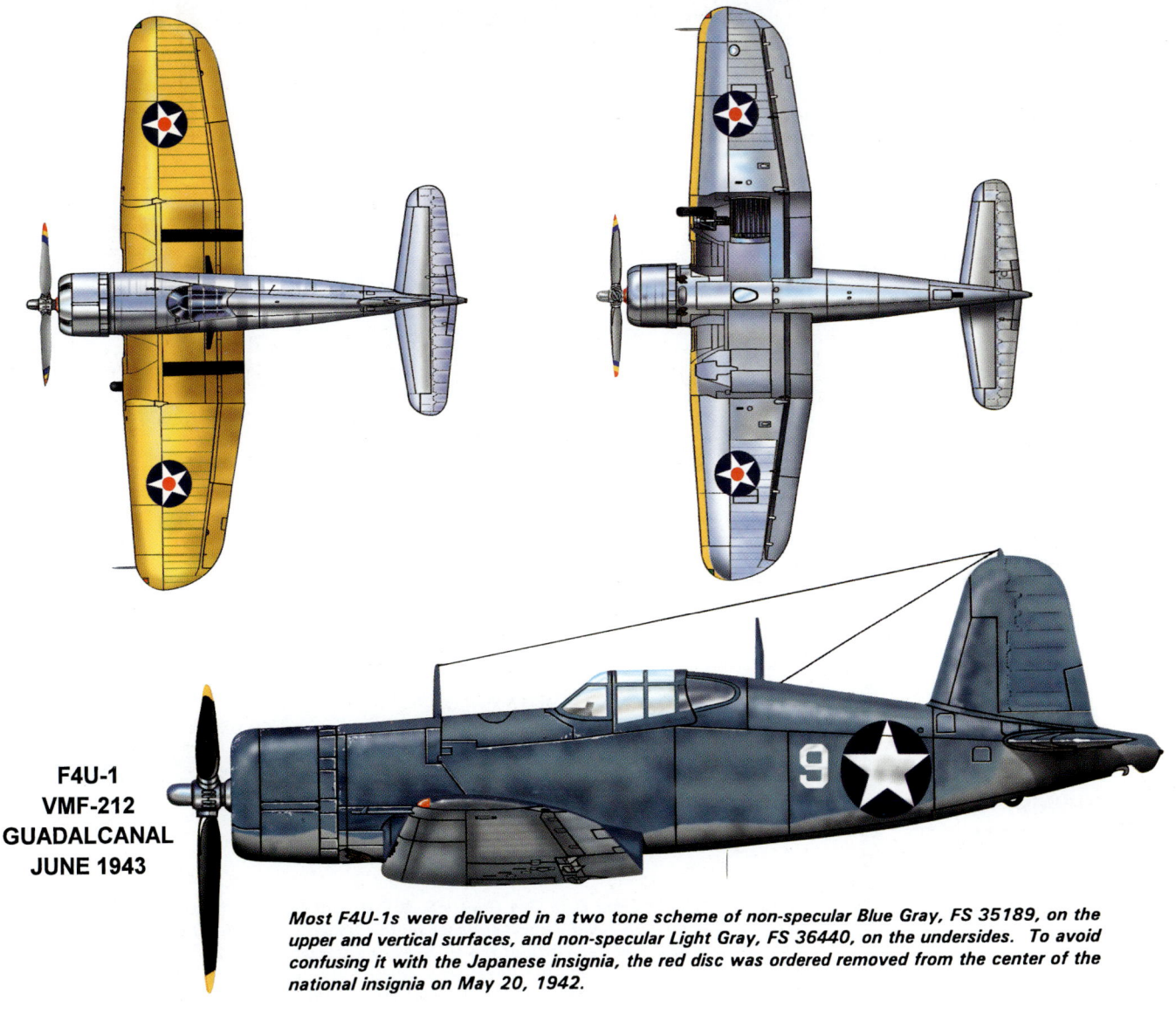

F4U-1 VMF-212 GUADALCANAL JUNE 1943

Most F4U-1s were delivered in a two tone scheme of non-specular Blue Gray, FS 35189, on the upper and vertical surfaces, and non-specular Light Gray, FS 36440, on the undersides. To avoid confusing it with the Japanese insignia, the red disc was ordered removed from the center of the national insignia on May 20, 1942.

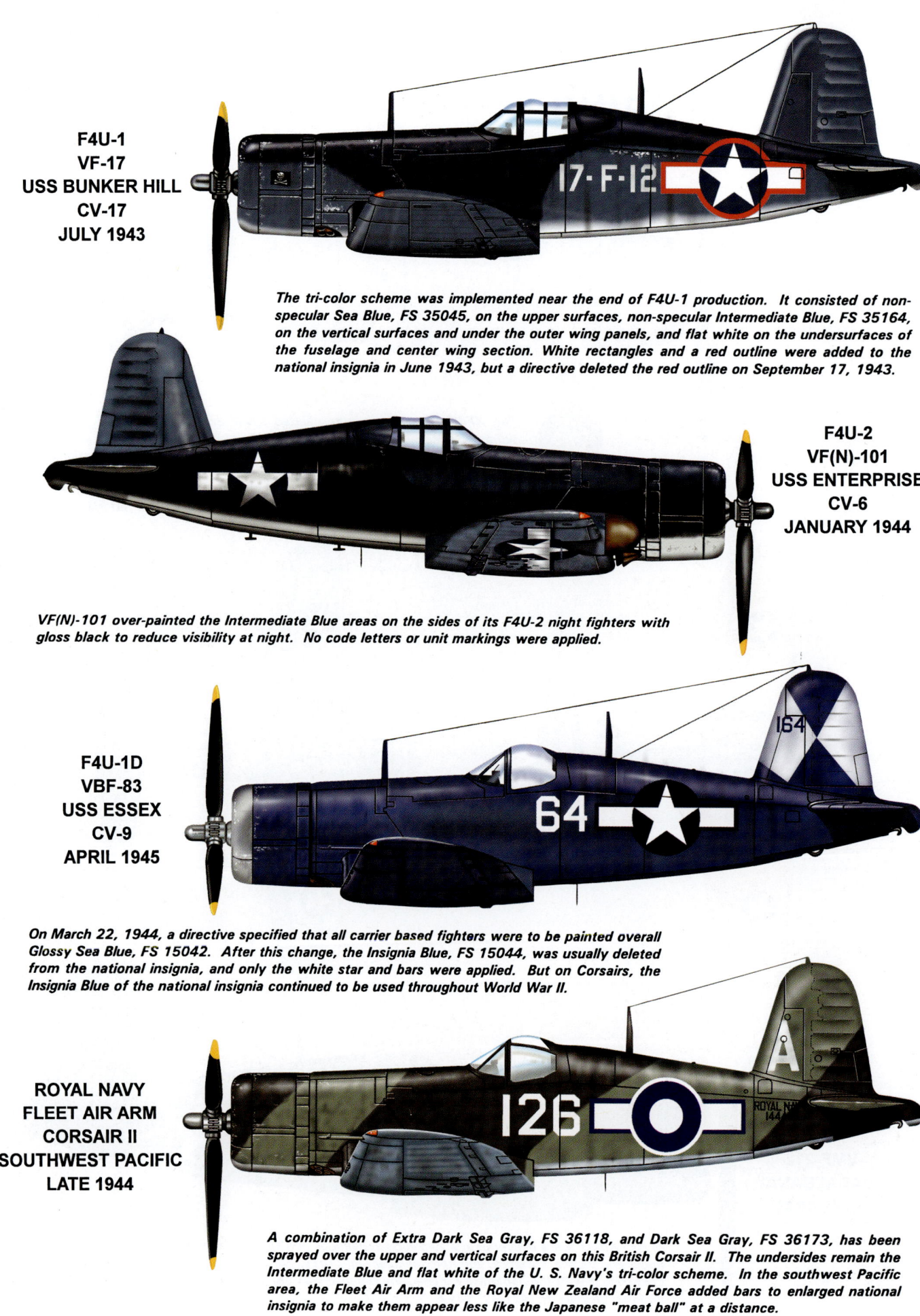

**F4U-1
VF-17
USS BUNKER HILL
CV-17
JULY 1943**

The tri-color scheme was implemented near the end of F4U-1 production. It consisted of non-specular Sea Blue, FS 35045, on the upper surfaces, non-specular Intermediate Blue, FS 35164, on the vertical surfaces and under the outer wing panels, and flat white on the undersurfaces of the fuselage and center wing section. White rectangles and a red outline were added to the national insignia in June 1943, but a directive deleted the red outline on September 17, 1943.

**F4U-2
VF(N)-101
USS ENTERPRISE
CV-6
JANUARY 1944**

VF(N)-101 over-painted the Intermediate Blue areas on the sides of its F4U-2 night fighters with gloss black to reduce visibility at night. No code letters or unit markings were applied.

**F4U-1D
VBF-83
USS ESSEX
CV-9
APRIL 1945**

On March 22, 1944, a directive specified that all carrier based fighters were to be painted overall Glossy Sea Blue, FS 15042. After this change, the Insignia Blue, FS 15044, was usually deleted from the national insignia, and only the white star and bars were applied. But on Corsairs, the Insignia Blue of the national insignia continued to be used throughout World War II.

**ROYAL NAVY
FLEET AIR ARM
CORSAIR II
SOUTHWEST PACIFIC
LATE 1944**

A combination of Extra Dark Sea Gray, FS 36118, and Dark Sea Gray, FS 36173, has been sprayed over the upper and vertical surfaces on this British Corsair II. The undersides remain the Intermediate Blue and flat white of the U. S. Navy's tri-color scheme. In the southwest Pacific area, the Fleet Air Arm and the Royal New Zealand Air Force added bars to enlarged national insignia to make them appear less like the Japanese "meat ball" at a distance.

This early F4U-1 is right off the production line, and it shows the original paint scheme applied to Corsairs. It consisted of non-specular Blue-Gray (FS 35189) over non-specular Light Gray (FS 36440). Almost all F4U-1s were delivered in this scheme, although a few had the later tri-color scheme. As delivered, most had the Insignia Blue disc and white star national insignia without the red disc in the center. This excellent photo provides very accurate values for the colors before they faded because of exposure to the elements. Typical flying gear worn by Corsair pilots is also illustrated. The bomb rack under the wing is natural metal. (NMNA)

Color photographs taken of Corsairs during World War II are surprisingly rare. This F4U-1A was assigned to VMF-214's Black Sheep on Espiritu Santo, and it illustrates how the colors faded from exposure to the elements in the South Pacific. This exposure, along with repainting in the field, often resulted in an appearance that was quite unlike a freshly painted tri-color scheme of non-specular Sea Blue (FS 35045), non-specular Intermediate Blue (FS 35164), and flat white. This Corsair retains the original blue disc and white star insignia without the bars on the sides. (NMNA)

During their service in World War II, Corsairs were more commonly found operating from island bases rather than from the decks of aircraft carriers. Palm trees formed the backdrop rather than shipboard superstructures, antennas, and gun mounts. Marine and Navy personnel, often stripped to the waist, toiled in the hot sun and monsoon rains to keep the aircraft maintained and armed for combat. This typical scene was repeated countless times as American forces battled across the islands of the Pacific. Note the mission markings on the aircraft to the right. The later style national insignia, with the bars on the side, is applied to these aircraft. (NMNA)

CORSAIR DETAILS IN COLOR
F4U-1A COCKPIT DETAILS & COLORS

Although the gun sight has been removed, the cockpit in the FG-1A on display at the Marine Corps Museum in Quantico, Virginia, remains very much as it was when the aircraft was in service. Details and colors of the instrument panel are illustrated here. The cockpit in an F4U-1A or an F3A-1A would be the same as the one in this early production FG-1A. Note the "eyebrow" armament panel which is mounted on the left side above the main instrument panel.

None of the "dash 1" Corsairs had floors in the cockpit. This design was originally intended to permit the pilot to see out of the window in the bottom of the fuselage. But the window was subsequently deleted, and Corsair variants beginning with the F4U-4 had solid floors in the cockpit. Instead of a floor, the F4U-1 through the F4U-1D had two foot troughs just below the rudder pedals.

The interior of the cockpit was painted with Chromate Green Primer, but the consoles were flat black. This is the console on the right side of the cockpit.

The headrest and the operating mechanism for the canopy are illustrated in this view.

Engine controls were on the quadrant above the left console, while the trim wheels and fuel selector switch can be seen on the console itself.

F4U-1D/FG-1D COCKPIT DETAILS & COLORS

The National Museum of Naval Aviation in Pensacola has a nicely restored FG-1D on display, and the photographs on this page were taken in its cockpit. Although one instrument and the "eyebrow" armament panel are missing, it otherwise closely represents most of the details found in the F4U-1D and FG-1D Corsairs.

Like the earlier F4U-1 and -1A, the F4U-1D and FG-1D did not have a floor in the cockpit, although the window in the bottom of the fuselage was not installed in any of the -D variants. This view shows the foot troughs and the rudder pedals to good effect. Also note the control column in the center of the photograph. The vent for cockpit cooling air is up under the instrument panel between the two foot troughs.

Many Corsairs were delivered with cockpit side panels that were painted flat black, and this FG-1D is one of them. Details on the left side of the cockpit are illustrated here.

The right console had various switches for electrical equipment.

Details of the seat are visible here. Note the colors and widths of the shoulder harness straps and the lap belts.

This close-up shows details of the right rudder pedal and foot trough as well as some of the plumbing up under the instrument panel in the forward area of the cockpit.

37

FUSELAGE DETAILS

Originally, the F4U-1 had cowl flaps all the way around the fuselage. The top flaps were soon fixed in the closed position to prevent oil from blowing back onto the windscreen. By the time the F4U-1D was produced, this permanent panel had replaced those flaps.

The filler for the main fuel tank was located on top of the fuselage a little forward of the windscreen. The stenciling reads FUEL, 100 OCT., 237 GAL.

The open cowl flaps and exhausts on the right side of the aircraft are shown here. All F4U-1 variants had six exhausts which were grouped in threes on each side of the lower fuselage. All subsequent production variants had some of their exhaust ports located above each wing.

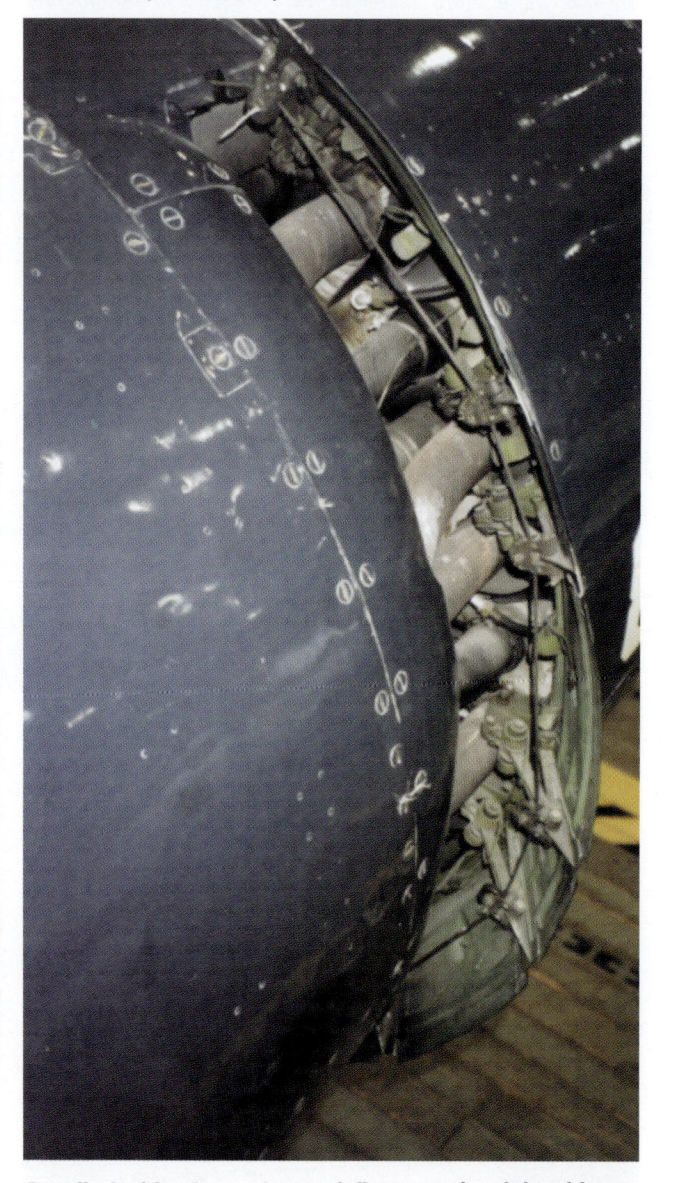

Details inside the open cowl flaps on the right side are revealed in this view. These include the actuating mechanism for the flaps as well as part of the exhaust manifold.

All F4U-1 variants had a windscreen with a curved front glass. This was also used on initial F4U-4 versions as well, but it was changed to one with a flat front glass for most F4U-4s and subsequent production variants. Also note the hand hold next to the windscreen. Another hand hold was located in the same position on the opposite side.

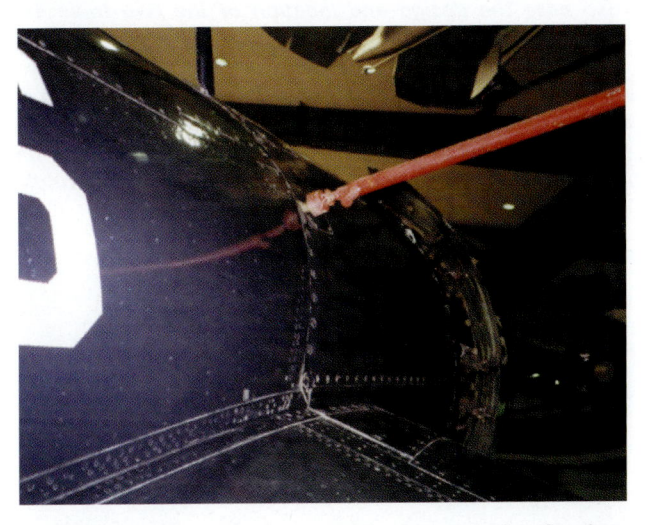

Corsairs could have one, two, or no antenna masts depending on the radio gear that was installed. This close-up shows how the antenna wire running from the leading edge of the vertical stabilizer was attached to the top of the forward antenna mast. Masts of at least two different heights were used in this forward location.

A fitting was present on both sides of the fuselage. When the wings were in the folded position, one end of a red brace was attached to the fitting as shown here, while the other end was placed in a similar fitting on the top of the wing. (See page 45.)

Although the semi-bubble canopy with the lateral frames was fitted to early F4U-1Ds, a change was made during production to this clear-vision canopy with no frames. Also note the aft antenna mast in this photograph.

A blue light was located on the spine of the aircraft.

The circular panel just above the R and the I in MARINES was a removable panel that covered the hoist tube. This tube ran all the way through the aft fuselage, and a lifting bar could be placed through it to hoist the rear of the aircraft up for maintenance or for boresighting the guns.

39

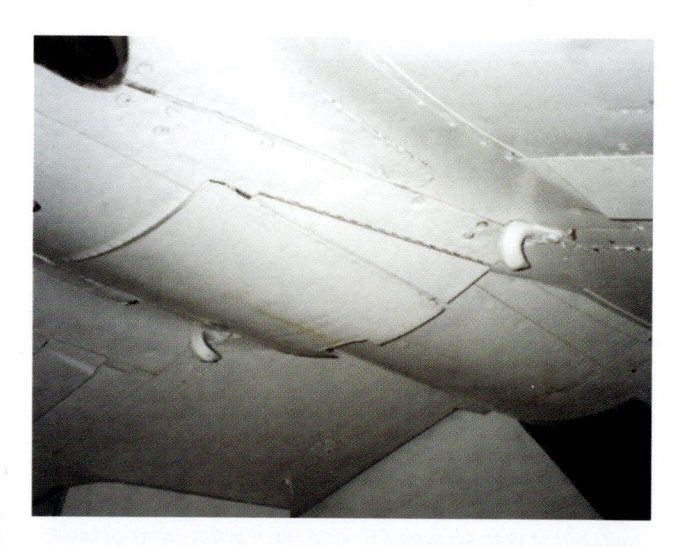

Left: The underside of the forward fuselage is shown here. Notice how the cowl flaps went all the way around the bottom of the fuselage. The vent door for engine compartment cooling can be seen in the open position. Also note the design and location of the two triple exhaust ports.

Above: The vent door for engine compartment cooling is shown here again from the left side. Also noteworthy are the two catapult hooks. Whenever the Corsair was to be launched from a carrier by catapult, one end of the bridle would be attached to each of these hooks.

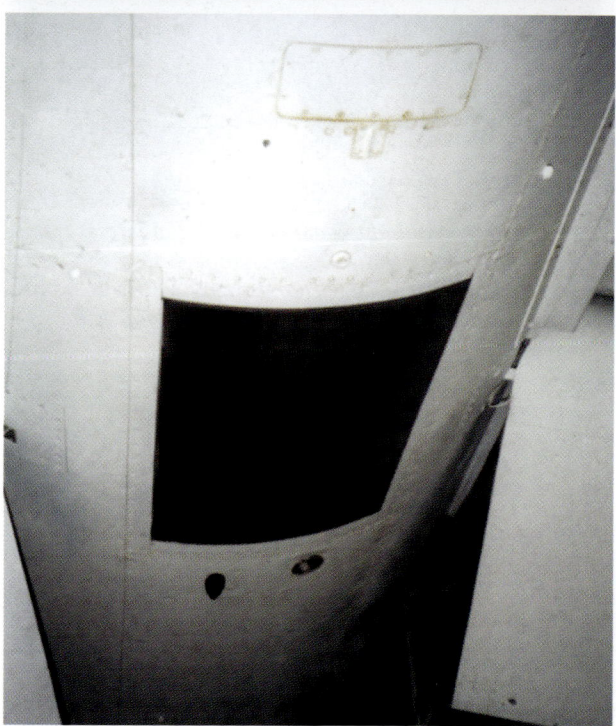

Early Corsairs, including all F4U-1s and some F4U-1As, had a window in the bottom of the fuselage. But it proved impractical, and it was subsequently deleted. The window was also painted over on many of the aircraft which had it. This one is on an early FG-1A.

A whip antenna was located under the aft fuselage on many F4U-1Ds, but there were few other details in this area.

40

WING DETAILS

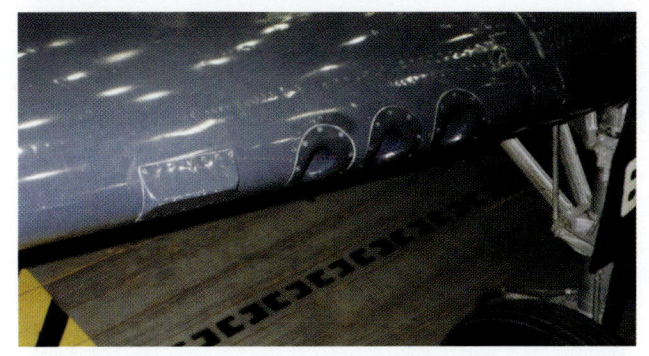

A small spoiler was added to the leading edge of the right wing just outboard of the three gun ports. This spoiler was one of the fixes for the carrier landing problems experienced with early Corsairs when the left wing tended to stall before the right wing. This spoiler was also retrofitted to earlier versions which were produced before it became a production standard.

This underside view of the left wing shows the three shell ejector slots for the machine guns and the four sets of zero-length rocket launchers. These rocket launchers became standard during production of the F4U-1D. The outer door for the left main landing gear is to the right in the photograph.

Above: The pitot probe was located on the leading edge of the left wing near the tip. It remained the same for all F4U-1 through F4U-1D versions.

Right: The black area on top of the wing was a spring loaded panel that served as a step. Another step, which was also covered by a spring loaded panel, can be seen on the side of the fuselage. Also note the rib on the fuselage where the flap fits when it is in the closed position.

The intake in the right wing root is shown here. The oil cooler was at the outer end of the intake, while vanes on the inner two-thirds of the intake directed the airflow into the aft engine compartment.

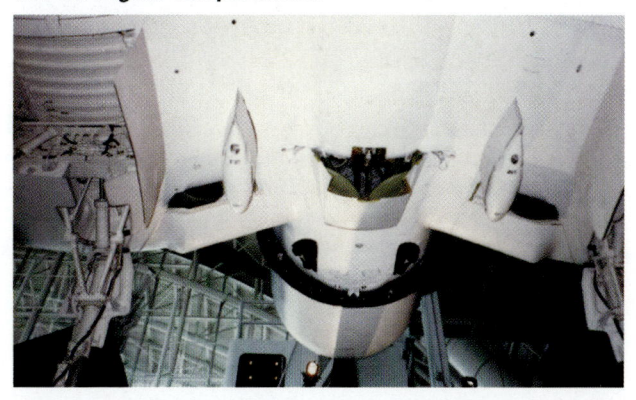

The two pylons that first appeared on the F4U-1D can be seen here, and they have their aerodynamic covers in place. Also note the open vents for the oil coolers just forward of the pylons.

41

WING LIGHTS

Three identification lights were located on the underside of the right wing near the tip. They were red, green, and amber from front to rear, although the green light appeared to be dark blue when it was not illuminated. These lights were eliminated from some later Corsair variants.

All Corsairs through the F4U-1D and FG-1D had a blue formation light mounted flush with the top of each outer wing panel. The white, teardrop shaped, recognition light was on the top of the right wing only. It was on all F4U-1s, FG-1s, F3A-1s, F4U-1As, and FG-1As. It was also on early F4U-1Ds and FG-1Ds, but it was deleted beginning with F4U-1D, BuNo. 57484, and FG-1D, BuNo. 87988. Also note the hand hold at the very bottom of the photo. It is covered with a spring loaded panel.

Navigation lights on the wing tips were mounted under triangular shaped covers. The covers were clear, and the light had the appropriate colored bulb under the cover.

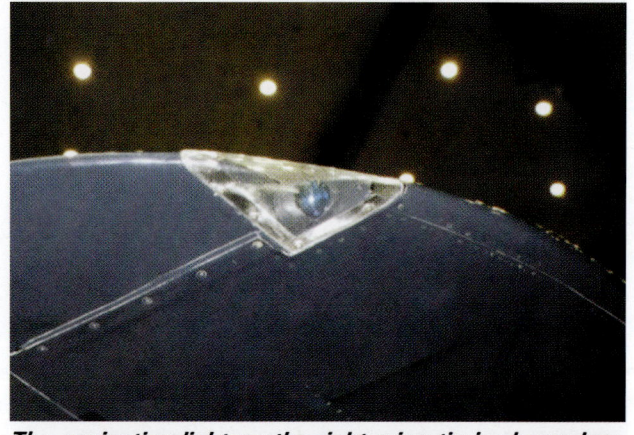

The navigation light on the right wing tip is shown here from the underside. The light was green, but it appeared to be blue when it was not illuminated.

This is the red light on the left wing tip as seen from slightly above.

This underside view reveals additional details of the navigation light on the tip of the left wing.

AILERON DETAILS

The underside of the right aileron is shown here. Note the three small fairings near the leading edge.

The left aileron had two tabs. These included the one at the inboard end and a second one further outboard on the trailing edge.

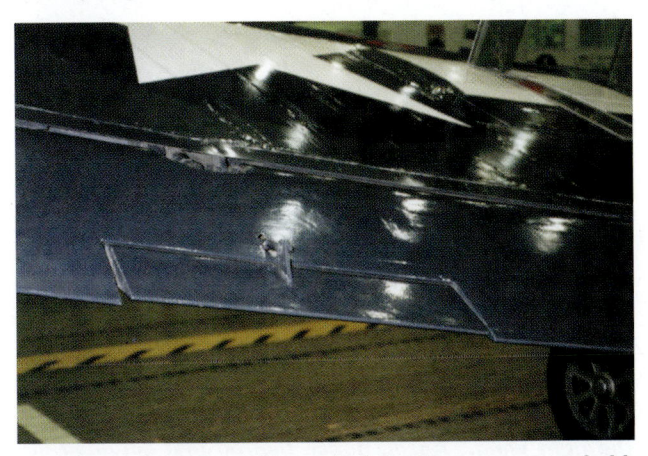

Details of the outer tab on the left aileron are revealed in this view. The actuating arm was on the top.

There was only one tab on the right aileron, and it was located at the inboard end of the trailing edge. The ailerons, like much of the outer wing sections, were covered with fabric.

This close-up provides a detailed look at the tab on the right aileron.

This close-up shows details of the inner tab and its actuator on the left aileron.

43

FLAP DETAILS

Because of the design of the inverted gull wing and the fact that the wings had to fold, the flaps on each side were designed in three different sections. These are the flaps on the left wing.

With the wings in the folded position, the outer edge of the center flap on the right wing can be seen along with its actuating rod which is located within the wing fold hinge area.

The inner and center flap sections on the right wing are illustrated here. Note the spanner that covered the gap between the two sections. The cut out step in the inner flap section was only on the right side, and it was found on late F4U-1Ds and all F4U-4s. It was not a production standard on F4U-1s or F4U-1As, however, because the flaps were interchangeable, some of these earlier Corsairs may have had them fitted as replacements. The other two steps, including the one on top of the wing and the one in the side of the fuselage, are also visible.

Hinges for the flaps on the left wing can be seen in this photograph.

Here is a look at the underside of the outer flap section on the right wing. Again, notice the rod that actuated the flap and the hinges which connected it to the wing.

WING FOLD DETAILS

Details of the right wing fold hinge area are shown here. Note how the top of the forward part of the wing actually drops below the hinge line when the wing is folded.

The left wing fold hinge was essentially a mirror image of that on the right. Hydraulic lines, cylinders, and electrical wiring are all visible in this photograph.

When the wings were to be folded, a small door which covered the main hinge opened as shown here. This is the door on top of the left wing.

The same door is shown here after the wing has been folded.

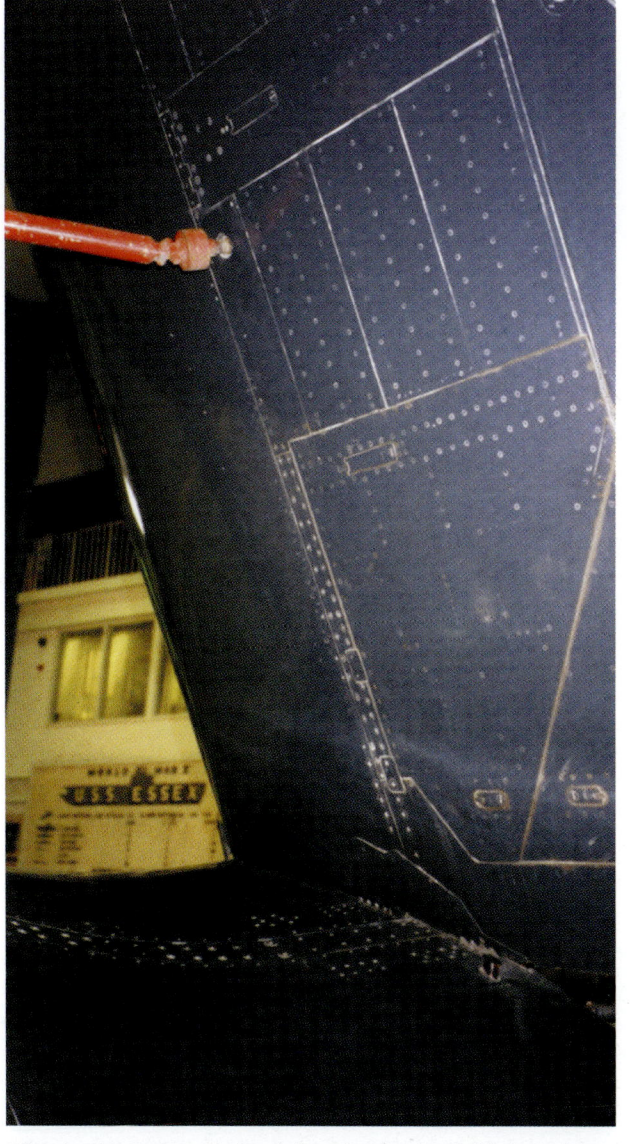

This is the inside of the right wing in the folded position. Again notice the location of the small door. The red brace has been installed between the top of the wing and the fuselage.

45

TAIL DETAILS
VERTICAL TAIL

Two-thirds of the Corsair's vertical tail was the movable rudder. The fixed vertical stabilizer was relatively small when compared to other aircraft designs.

On some Corsairs, one or two antenna wires were attached to the top of the vertical stabilizer as shown here. On other aircraft, the wires were attached to a stub mast at the top of the rudder. Depending on the radio equipment installed, one or two wires could be present, and in some cases there were none. When present, the wires ran from the vertical tail to the antenna masts, insulators located on the aft fuselage, or even to the right horizontal stabilizer.

A single trim tab was located at the bottom of the rudder's trailing edge. Note how the top edge of the tab was parallel to the ground line rather than the chord line of the vertical tail.

This left side view of the trim tab shows the actuating arm which was located at the top of the tab.

46

HORIZONTAL TAIL

An overall view of the left horizontal stabilizer and elevator is provided here. Like the rudder and ailerons, the elevators were fabric covered. The round access panels were on the top of the left horizontal stabilizer.

Here is a look at the entire upper surface on the right horizontal stabilizer and elevator. Notice that the round access panels are not present on the top. Instead, they are located on the bottom. This was because the two horizontal tails were interchangeable, and these access panels were only on one side.

The tab arrangement on the elevators was unusual, and each elevator had a split tab arrangement. These are the tabs on the left elevator, and the outer portion is operated by a short actuator on top.

The inner part of the left tab was controlled by a long arm that was connected to the underside of the horizontal stabilizer.

Because the left and right horizontal tails were interchangeable, the tab arrangement on the right elevator was the reverse of that on the left. A long hinged arm connected the outer tab to the top of the horizontal stabilizer.

The inner tab had the smaller actuator on the underside of the elevator. Several of the round access panels are visible on the underside of the horizontal stabilizer.

47

R-2800 ENGINE DETAILS & COLORS

An R-2800-8W engine is seen here installed in an FG-1D.

This front view provides a good look at the details of the gear reduction housing and the front of the forward row of cylinders.

Above and right: Details on the right side of an R-2800 are revealed in the photograph above, while the left side and the aft end of the engine can be seen at right.

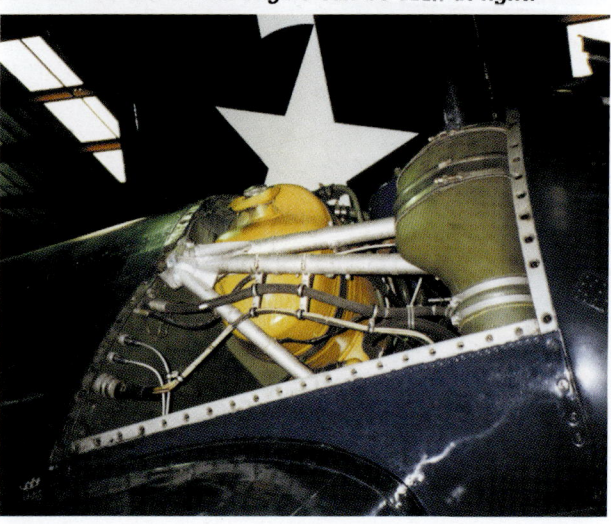

Above and left: Details and colors inside the engine accessory compartment are shown in these two photos.

48

F4U-1A ARMAMENT IMPROVISIONS

The small bomb racks initially installed under the wings of the F4U-1 did not prove practical, so a special rack was developed by Brewster to carry bombs up to the 1000-pound size under the fuselage of the F4U-1A. A developmental installation with a dummy 1000-pound bomb is shown here. This provision was on F4U-1As, BuNos. 17930 through 50349. (Vought)

The rack had to be designed so that the cooling vent for the engine accessory compartment would have clearance to operate. Here, the rack is shown installed, and the cooling vent is open. Compare this with the photo at left which shows the vent in the closed position. (Vought)

Several different designs for rocket installations were tested for the F4U-1A. A bolt-on set of launchers is seen here beneath the right wing. (Vought)

This is another look at the rocket launchers shown in the photo at left, but this time rockets have been loaded. Rockets were not carried operationally by the Corsair until the zero-length launchers for five-inch rockets became a standard feature on the F4U-1D. (Vought)

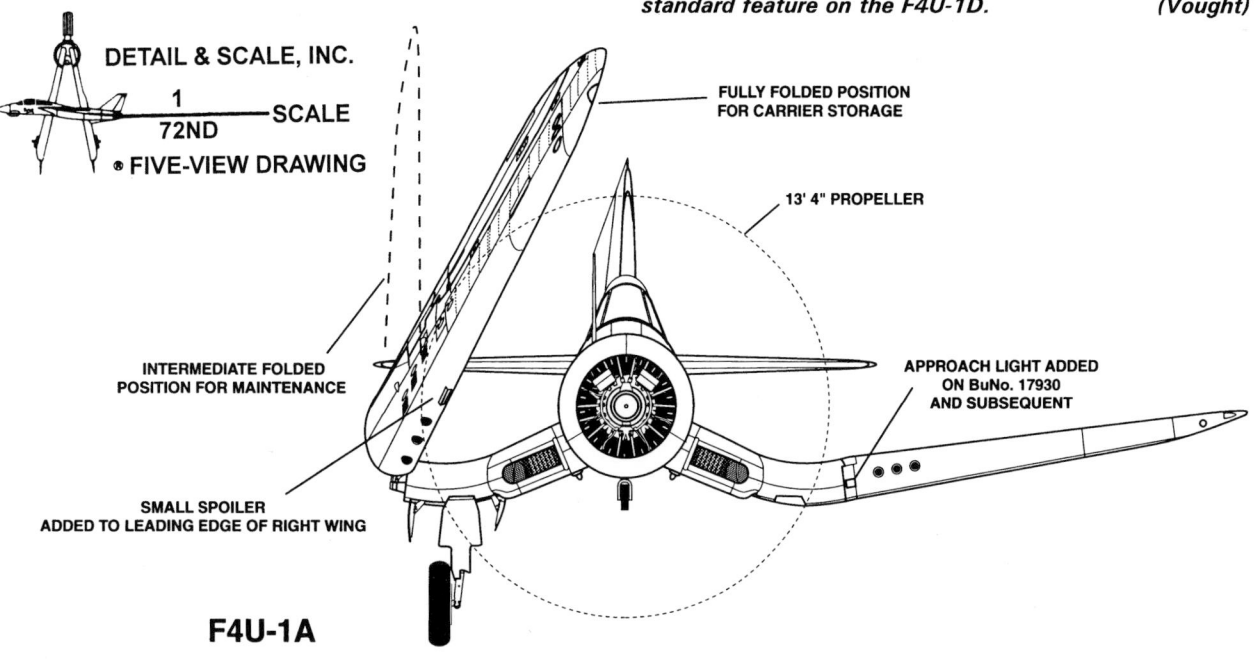

DETAIL & SCALE, INC.
1/72ND SCALE
FIVE-VIEW DRAWING

FULLY FOLDED POSITION FOR CARRIER STORAGE

13' 4" PROPELLER

INTERMEDIATE FOLDED POSITION FOR MAINTENANCE

APPROACH LIGHT ADDED ON BuNo. 17930 AND SUBSEQUENT

SMALL SPOILER ADDED TO LEADING EDGE OF RIGHT WING

F4U-1A

DETAIL & SCALE 1/72nd SCALE COPYRIGHT © DRAWING BY LLOYD S. JONES

DETAIL & SCALE, INC.
1/72ND SCALE
® FIVE-VIEW DRAWING

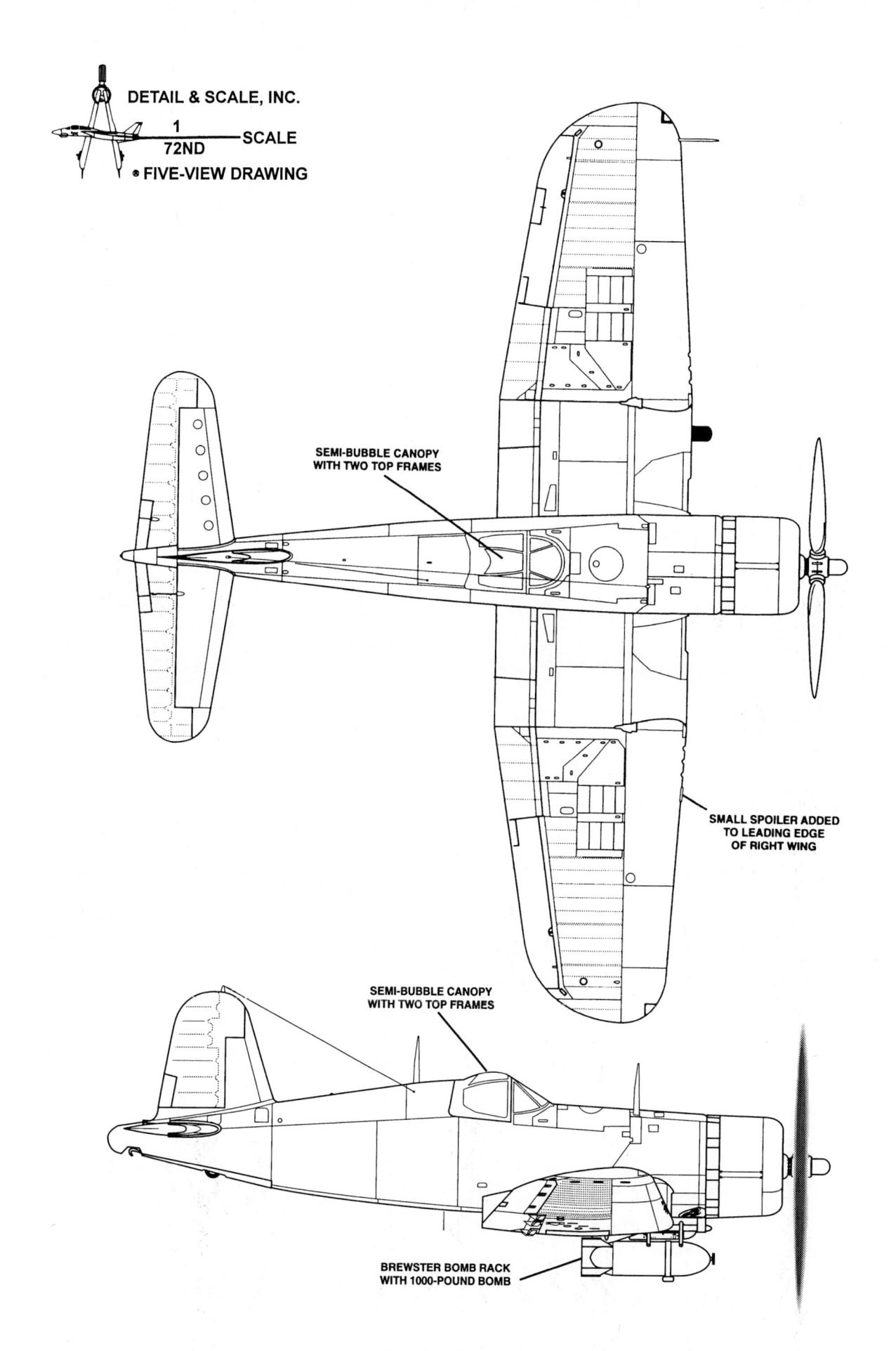

SEMI-BUBBLE CANOPY WITH TWO TOP FRAMES

SMALL SPOILER ADDED TO LEADING EDGE OF RIGHT WING

SEMI-BUBBLE CANOPY WITH TWO TOP FRAMES

BREWSTER BOMB RACK WITH 1000-POUND BOMB

DETAIL & SCALE 1/72nd SCALE COPYRIGHT © DRAWINGS BY LLOYD S. JONES

DETAIL & SCALE, INC.

1/72ND SCALE

FIVE-VIEW DRAWING

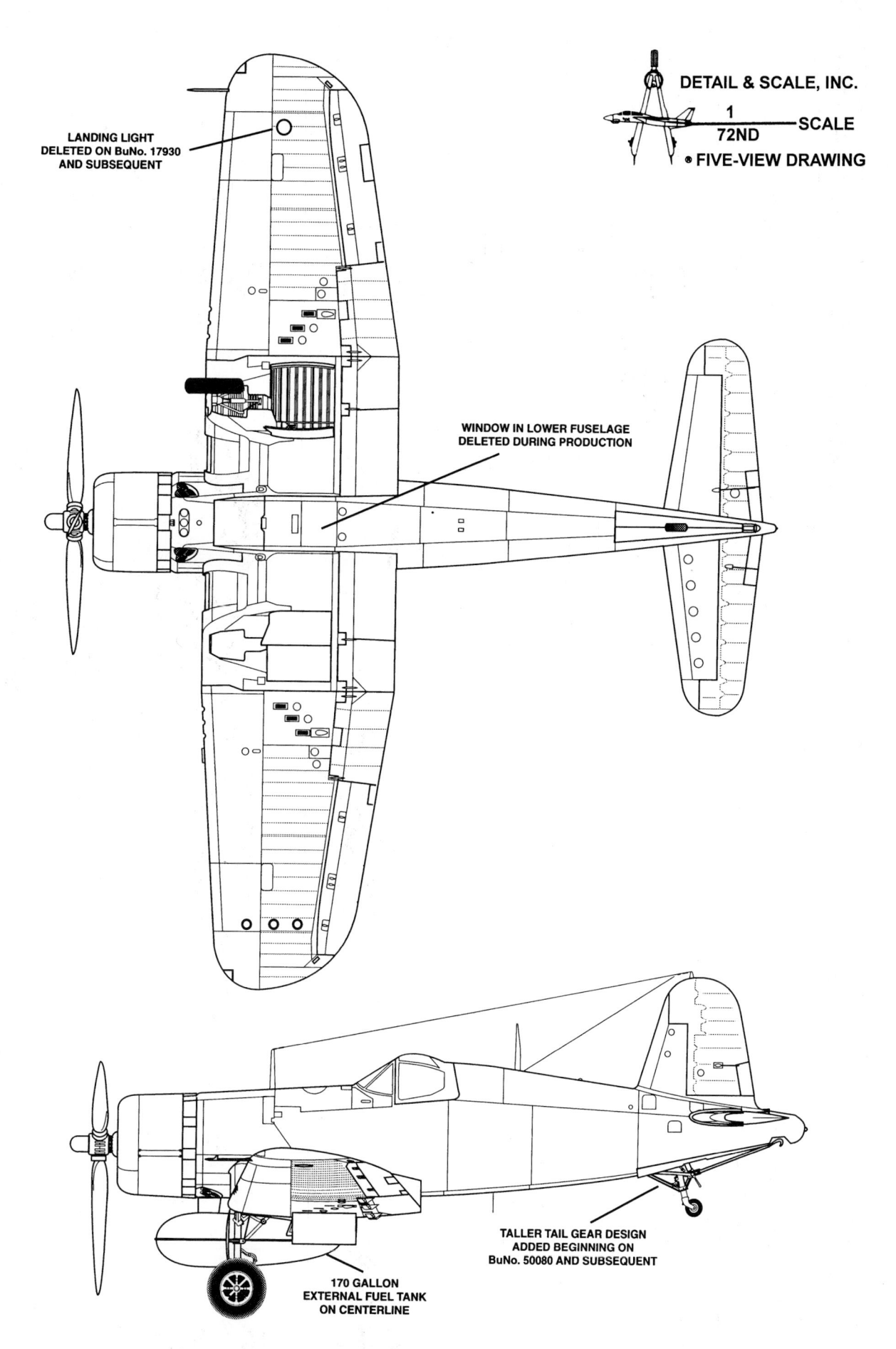

LANDING LIGHT DELETED ON BuNo. 17930 AND SUBSEQUENT

WINDOW IN LOWER FUSELAGE DELETED DURING PRODUCTION

TALLER TAIL GEAR DESIGN ADDED BEGINNING ON BuNo. 50080 AND SUBSEQUENT

170 GALLON EXTERNAL FUEL TANK ON CENTERLINE

DETAIL & SCALE 1/72nd SCALE COPYRIGHT © DRAWINGS BY LLOYD S. JONES

51

F4U-1C

The F4U-1C was the first cannon-armed Corsair variant. Four 20mm cannon replaced the six .50-caliber machine guns found in the other -1 variants. It was believed that the heavier shell and increased hitting power of the 20-mm cannon would be more effective against ground targets in particular. (Vought)

Some references on the Corsair have stated that the F4U-1C was essentially an F4U-1A armed with four 20-mm cannon instead of six .50-caliber machine guns. This is incorrect, because the F4U-1C was actually based on the F4U-1D airframe. The production of F4U-1Ds actually began before that of the F4U-1C, and thirteen blocks of F4U-1Ds were completed before the first group of F4U-1Cs began to alternate on the production line with the F4U-1Ds. Only 200 F4U-1Cs were built, and they were produced in small batches between F4U-1D blocks. All were built by Vought, and there were no equivalents produced by Goodyear or Brewster.

The hitting power of the 20-mm cannon was unquestionably higher than that of a .50-caliber machine gun, but less ammunition could be carried for the larger weapons. A total of 924 rounds were loaded for the four cannon as compared to 2,400 rounds for the six .50-caliber machine guns in the other "dash 1" variants. Most pilots preferred the extra ammunition and the resulting longer duration of fire over the heavier projectile of the 20-mm cannon.

Like the F4U-1D, the F4U-1C had the two pylons under the center wing section that could be used to carry bombs, napalm, or 154-gallon fuel tanks. When the rocket launch stubs were added with F4U-1D, BuNo. 82253, the next F4U-1C produced, BuNo. 82260, also had provisions for rockets installed. However, only two rockets could be carried under each wing of the F4U-1C, as compared to four on the F4U-1D. The 63-gallon leading edge wing tanks, found in the F4U-1 and F4U-1A, were deleted.

All F4U-1Cs were fitted with the smaller Hamilton-Standard propeller which had a diameter of 13' 1". All but the first three had the frameless clear-vision canopy that became standard on the F4U-1D on BuNo. 57583.

Although there were relatively few F4U-1Cs produced, they led the way for a number of later cannon-armed variants including the F4U-4B, all F4U-5 sub-variants, the F4U-7, and the AU-1.

All F4U-1Cs were delivered with propellers that were 13' 1" in diameter, and the taller tail wheel assembly was installed. A total of 924 rounds of ammunition was carried for the four 20-mm cannon. (Vought)

Above: The F4U-1C was produced with the clear-vision sliding canopy, and this feature was introduced on BuNo. 57777. This was essentially the same as the semi-bubble canopy used on the F4U-1A, however it did not have the two lateral frames at the top. It is shown here on an FG-1D. Most F4U-1Ds had the same canopy.

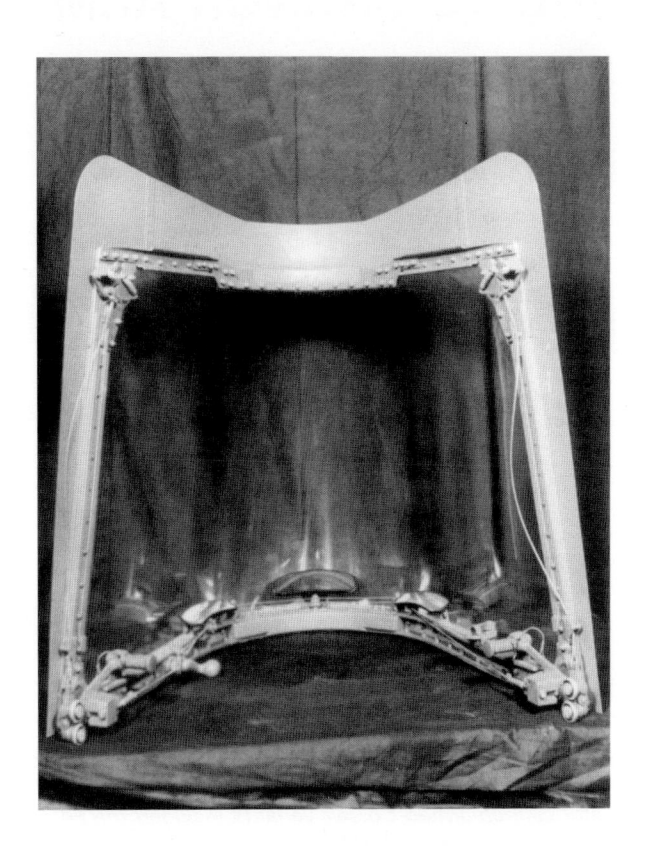

Right: Details on the inside of the clear-vision or frameless sliding canopy are shown in this view.   *(Vought)*

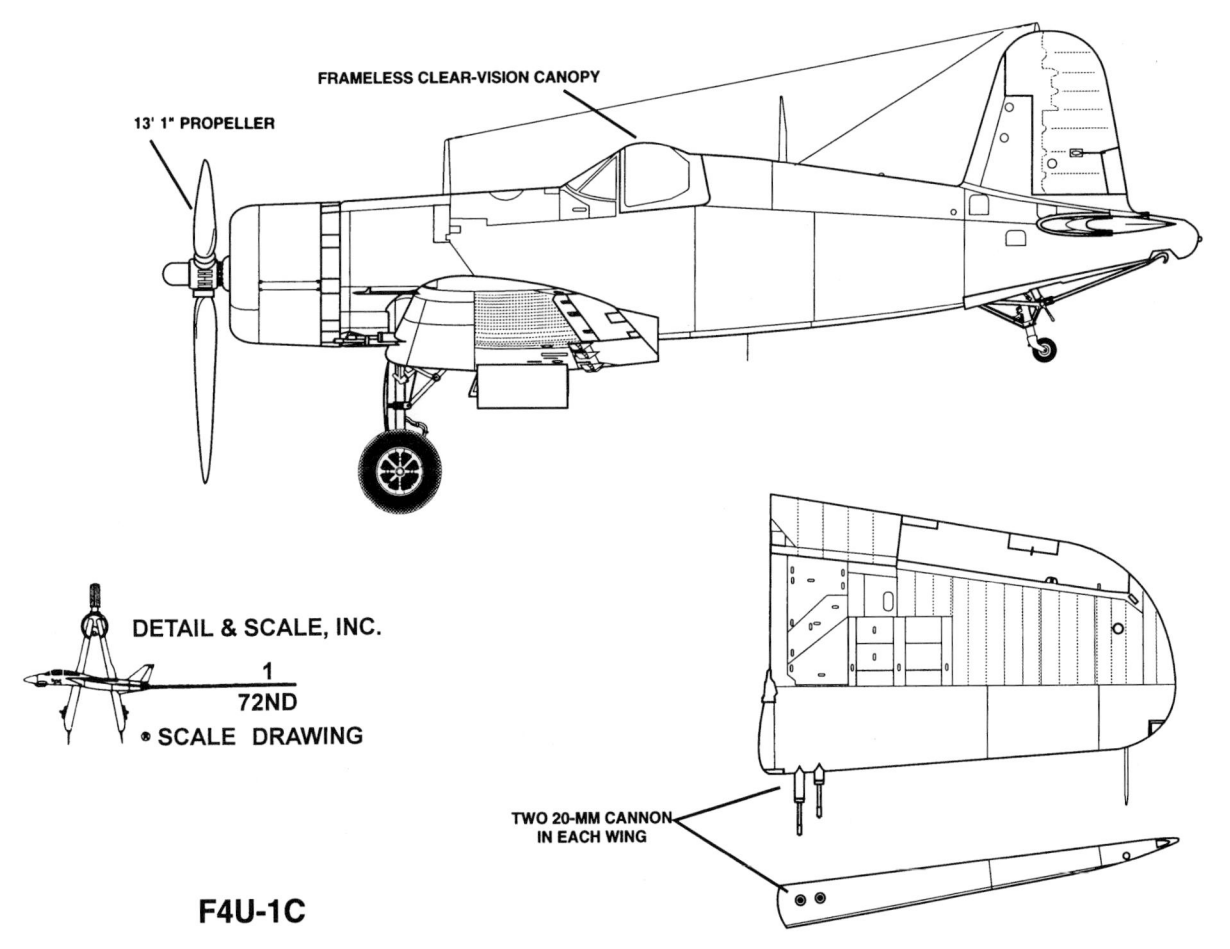

F4U-1C

FRAMELESS CLEAR-VISION CANOPY
13' 1" PROPELLER
TWO 20-MM CANNON IN EACH WING

DETAIL & SCALE, INC.
1/72ND SCALE DRAWING

DETAIL & SCALE 1/72nd SCALE COPYRIGHT © DRAWING BY LLOYD S. JONES

F4U-1C CANNON ARMAMENT

Above, left and right: The cannon installation in the left wing of an F4U-1C is illustrated in these two photographs. Only 200 F4U-1Cs were built by Vought, but later cannon-armed Corsair variants included the F4U-4B, F4U-5, AU-1, and F4U-7. *(Both Vought)*

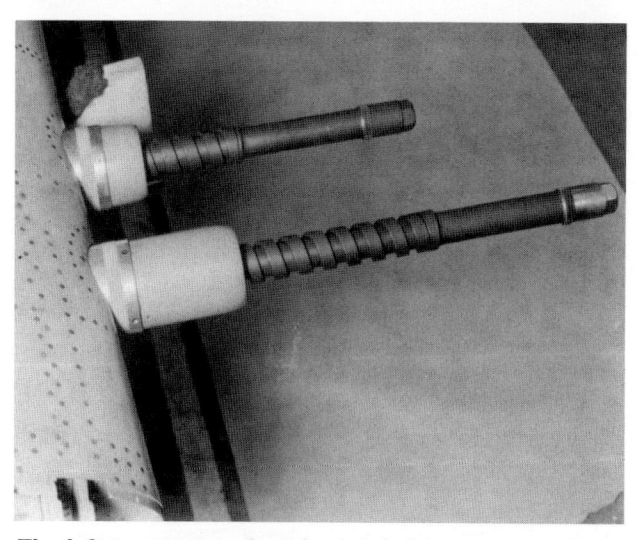

The left two cannon barrels and their mounts are shown here from above. The cannon barrels on the F4U-1C extended considerably further out in front of the leading edge of the wing than on any of the subsequent cannon-armed variants. (See *The F4U Corsair in Detail & Scale, Part 2,* for a look at the other cannon-armed Corsairs.) *(Vought)*

Right: The two mounts without the cannons installed can be seen here. Also note the small fairings on the top of the wing that provide clearance for the cannon installation. *(Vought)*

F4U-1D

The F4U-1D was the fighter-bomber version of the "dash one" series of Corsairs. The Goodyear equivalent was the FG-1D. These aricraft were fitted with two pylons under the wing center section, and these could be loaded with bombs, napalm, or external fuel tanks. Most F4U-1Ds and FG-1Ds also had four zero-length launchers under each wing for 5-inch rockets. Here an FG-1D from VMF-312 is loaded with bombs on Okinawa on April 17, 1945. (USN via NMNA)

Within the development of the Corsair, the F4U-1D reflected the trend to turn large fighters into capable fighter-bombers. As originally designed, the Corsair had little capability to carry external ordnance, but the need for such ability was recognized early on. Flying F4U-1s from their land bases in the Pacific, Marine and Navy pilots often wished they had more than their machine guns with which to attack numerous targets on the ground. This led to the development of the add-on Brewster bomb rack that was fitted to most F4U-1As. But with the F4U-1D, and its cannon armed equivalent, the F4U-1C, the fighter-bomber potential of the Corsair was finally realized.

Two pylons were added under the center wing section, and these could be used to carry bombs up to 1,000 pounds in size, napalm, or 154-gallon fuel tanks. Because of the increased ability to carry external fuel, the two 63-gallon leading edge fuel tanks in the wings were deleted.

A common misconception about the F4U-1D was that it was produced with the clear-vision canopy without the two overhead frames. The fact is that the change to this canopy did not occur until production of BuNo. 57583. By that time, 803 F4U-1Ds had been produced with the semi-bubble canopy with the two overhead frames.

A number of other visible changes occurred during production of the F4U-1D and FG-1D. Beginning with BuNo. 57356, the 13' 4" Hamilton-Standard propeller, used on all previous Corsairs, was replaced with a slightly smaller one with a 13' 1" diameter. Beginning with BuNo. 82253, the capability to carry four five-inch rockets under each wing was added. Also during production

The F4U-1D was also the first version of the Corsair to be deployed aboard carriers in considerable numbers. Both Navy and Marine squadrons began serving regular carrier assignments in early 1945. This new F4U-1D belongs to VMF-512, and it is shown here taxiing to the catapult aboard its carrier on June 2, 1945. Most F4U-1Ds were delivered in the overall glossy Sea Blue finish as seen here, but the gloss quickly faded with exposure to the elements. Note that the national insignias have an Insignia Blue surround and border. (USN via NMNA)

Large geometric markings adorn these Goodyear FG-1Ds which were assigned to VMF-213 aboard the USS SAIDOR, CVE-117. Beginning with BuNo. 57356, F4U-1Ds were delivered with propellers that were 13' 1" in diameter. This change to a smaller propeller was also made beginning with FG-1D, BuNo. 76149.
(USN via NMNA)

of the F4U-1D, a cut out step was added to the right inboard flap to facilitate entry to the cockpit. The teardrop shaped recognition light on the top of the right wing was deleted beginning with BuNo. 57484.

A few early F4U-1Ds were delivered in the tri-color paint scheme of Sea Blue, Intermediate Blue, and flat white. But almost all were finished in the overall glossy Sea Blue scheme. Usually the top of the forward fuselage was finished with flat paint to reduce glare for the pilot. As Navy aircraft were painted in the overall Sea Blue scheme, it became common to delete the Insignia Blue from the national insignia and apply only the white star and two side bars. But this was not done on the Corsairs. The Insignia Blue was used for the national insignia even on the overall Sea Blue aircraft.

Vought produced 1,685 F4U-1Ds, while Goodyear exceeded this number by completing 1,997 FG-1Ds.

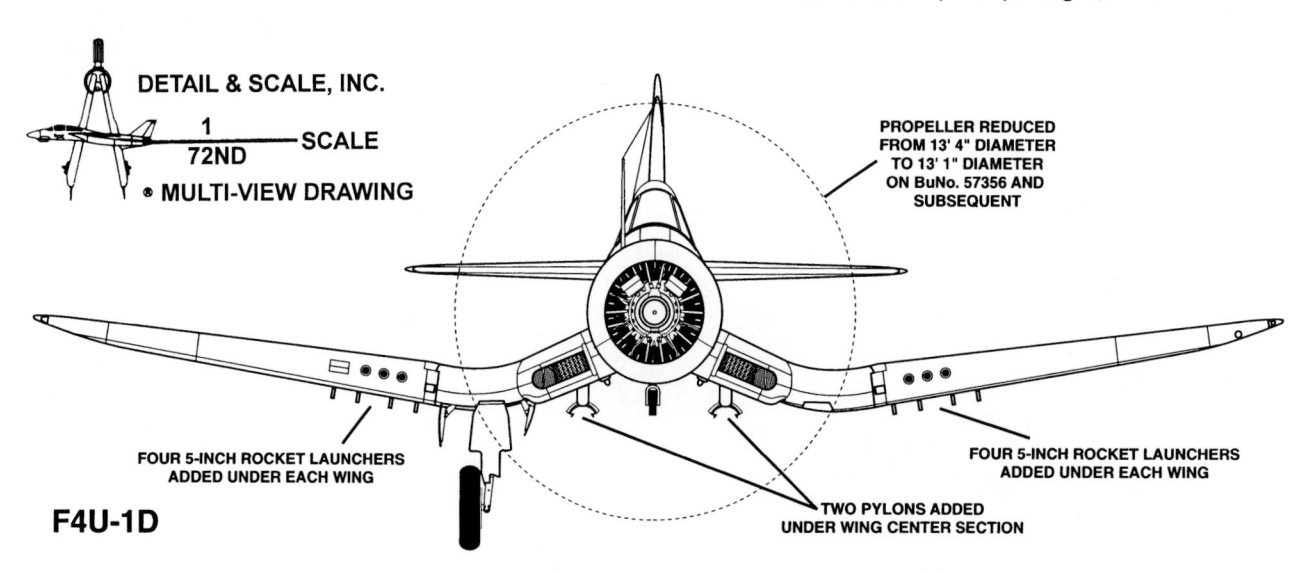

DETAIL & SCALE, INC.

1/72ND SCALE

® MULTI-VIEW DRAWING

PROPELLER REDUCED FROM 13' 4" DIAMETER TO 13' 1" DIAMETER ON BuNo. 57356 AND SUBSEQUENT

FOUR 5-INCH ROCKET LAUNCHERS ADDED UNDER EACH WING

FOUR 5-INCH ROCKET LAUNCHERS ADDED UNDER EACH WING

TWO PYLONS ADDED UNDER WING CENTER SECTION

F4U-1D

DETAIL & SCALE 1/72nd SCALE COPYRIGHT © DRAWING BY LLOYD S. JONES

DETAIL & SCALE, INC.
1/72ND SCALE
® MULTI-VIEW DRAWING

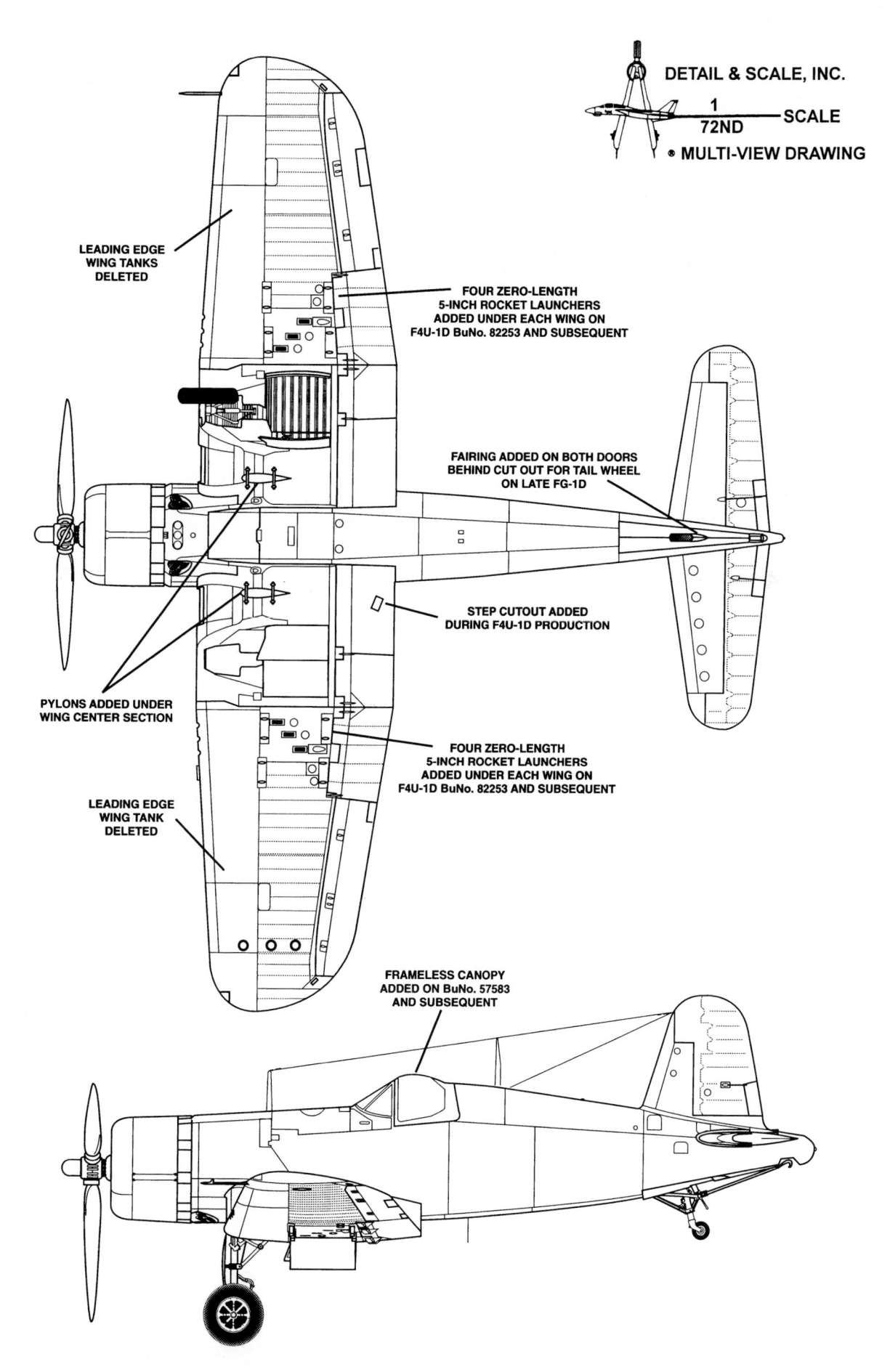

LEADING EDGE WING TANKS DELETED

FOUR ZERO-LENGTH 5-INCH ROCKET LAUNCHERS ADDED UNDER EACH WING ON F4U-1D BuNo. 82253 AND SUBSEQUENT

FAIRING ADDED ON BOTH DOORS BEHIND CUT OUT FOR TAIL WHEEL ON LATE FG-1D

STEP CUTOUT ADDED DURING F4U-1D PRODUCTION

PYLONS ADDED UNDER WING CENTER SECTION

FOUR ZERO-LENGTH 5-INCH ROCKET LAUNCHERS ADDED UNDER EACH WING ON F4U-1D BuNo. 82253 AND SUBSEQUENT

LEADING EDGE WING TANK DELETED

FRAMELESS CANOPY ADDED ON BuNo. 57583 AND SUBSEQUENT

DETAIL & SCALE 1/72nd SCALE COPYRIGHT © DRAWINGS BY LLOYD S. JONES

EXTERNAL STORES

Above: The F4U-1D had two pylons under the wing center section that were located just aft of the vent doors for the oil cooler intakes. This is the pylon on the right side, and the vent door can be seen just forward of the pylon. A protective fairing covered the bottom of the pylon when no external store was attached. *(Vought)*

Above right: Here is a look at the left pylon without the protective cover in place. *(Vought)*

Right: The pylons were also wet, which means that they had internal fuel lines to enable them to utilize external fuel tanks. In this photograph, the fuel tank is on the right pylon and a bomb is on the left. This same style tank was also filled with napalm, fitted with a fuse, and used as an effective weapon against the Japanese. The increased ability to carry external fuel resulted in the leading edge wing tanks being deleted from the F4U-1D. These internal fuel tanks had been on all previous production variants. *(Vought)*

Below: Even with bombs attached to the two pylons, a centerline fuel tank could also be fitted. *(Vought)*

ROCKET ARMAMENT

Left: In the last two years of World War II, rockets became more important as weapons for use against ground targets. Accordingly, the capability to carry rockets was added to more and more USAAF, Navy, and USMC aircraft as the war progressed. Beginning with F4U-1D, BuNo. 82253, and FG-1D, BuNo, 87788, four zero-length rocket launchers were added under each wing to carry five-inch high velocity aerial (HVAR) rockets. This capability was also added to some earlier Corsairs. (Vought)

Below, left and right: The rocket installation under the right wing is illustrated at left, while the rockets under the left wing are shown in the photograph at right.

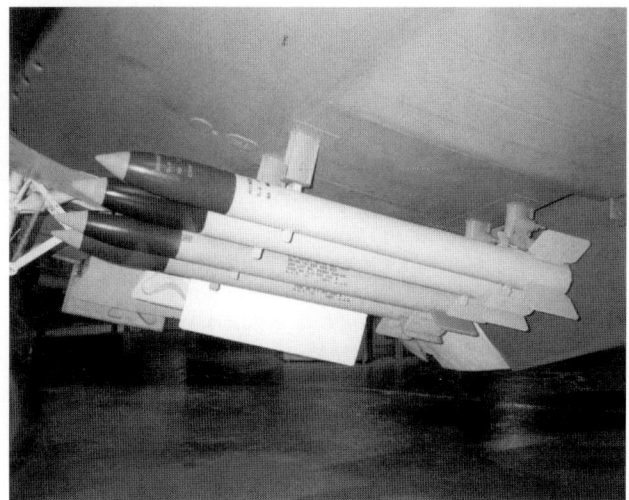

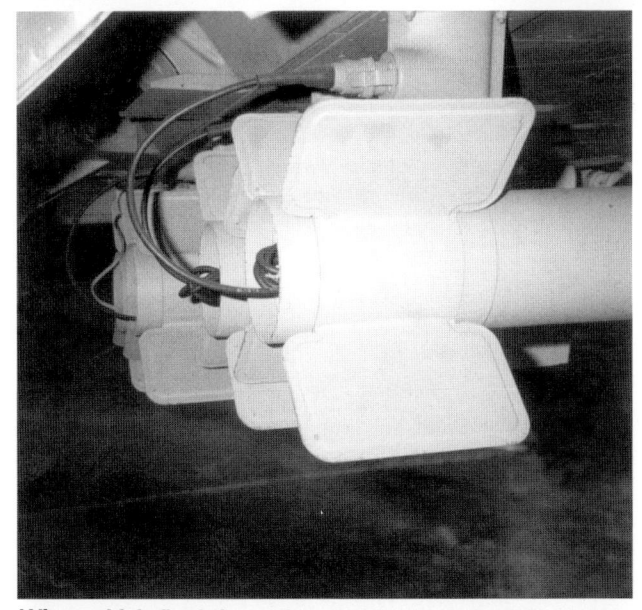

Wires which fired the rockets were attached to the trailing edge of each rear launch stub and connected inside the aft end of the rocket motor.

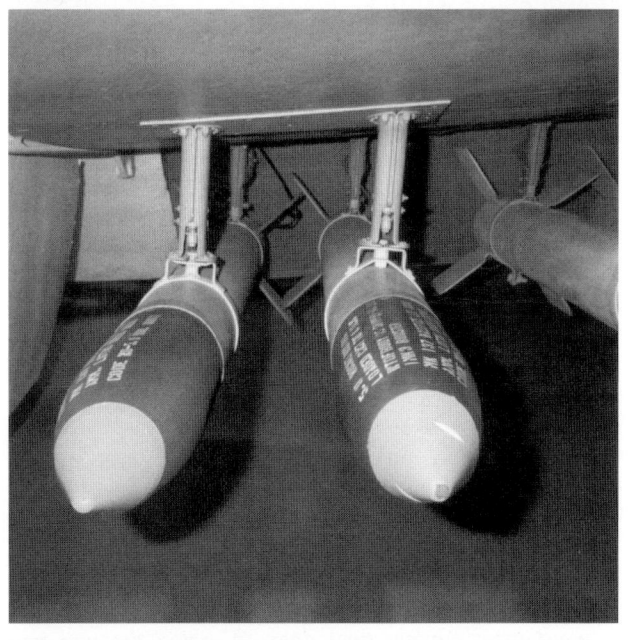

This front view illustrates how the rockets were attached to the forward launch stubs.

59

LANDING GEAR DETAILS
LEFT MAIN LANDING GEAR

Details on the inside of the left main landing gear are shown here. Note the hydraulic line running down the strut. Many Corsairs had landing gear struts that were a light gray as shown here, while photographs also show that some were a steel color, and others were painted the same color as the underside of the aircraft. This light gray color appears to have been used extensively on many early aircraft through the F4U-1A. (Vought)

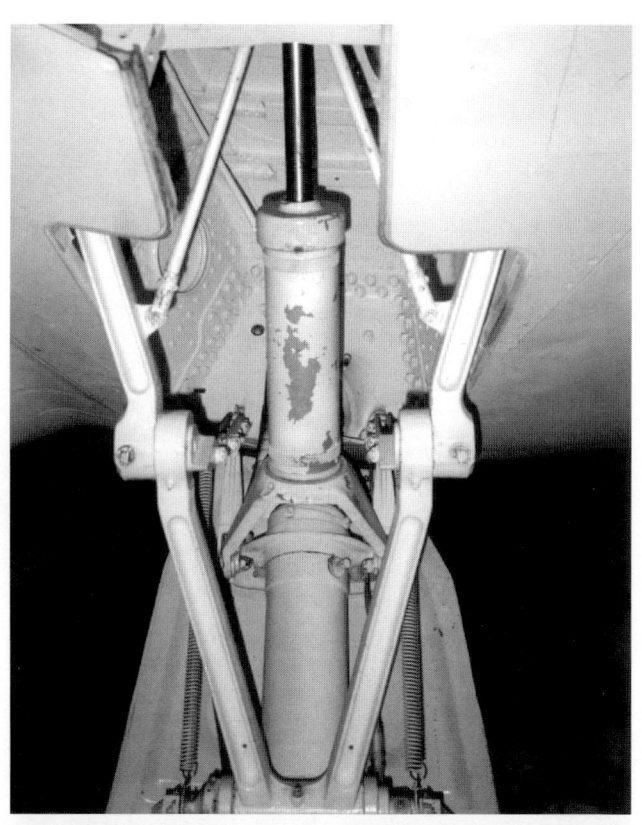

This view looks up and forward into the left main gear well and shows the hydraulic cylinder which extended and retracted the gear.

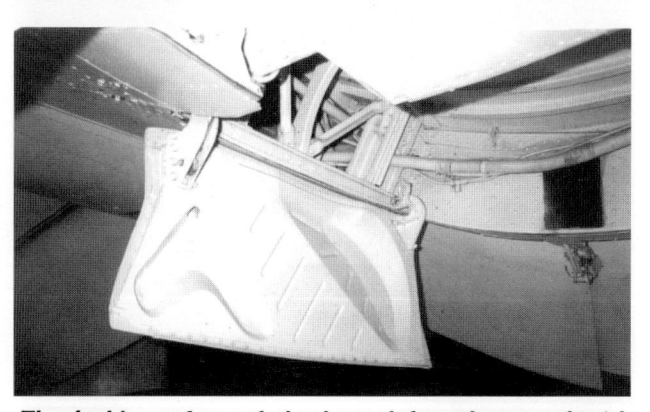

The inside surface of the inner left main gear door is shown here. The inner surfaces of the doors were usually painted the same color as the underside of the fuselage.

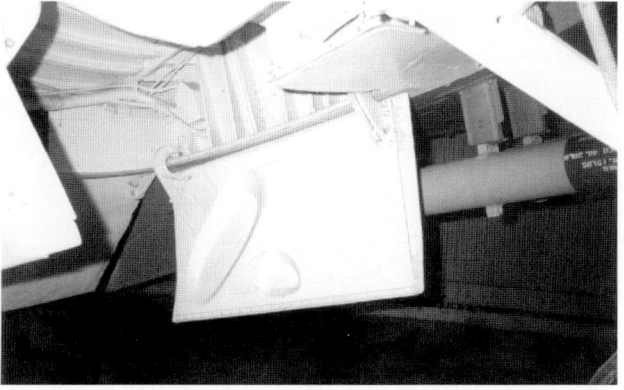

A small flexible covering was located at the top of each forward main landing gear door. It sealed the gap between the door and the wing when the door was closed.

This is the outer door on the left main landing gear.

60

RIGHT MAIN LANDING GEAR

Details of the main gear wheel are illustrated here. This is the right main gear as viewed from the outside.

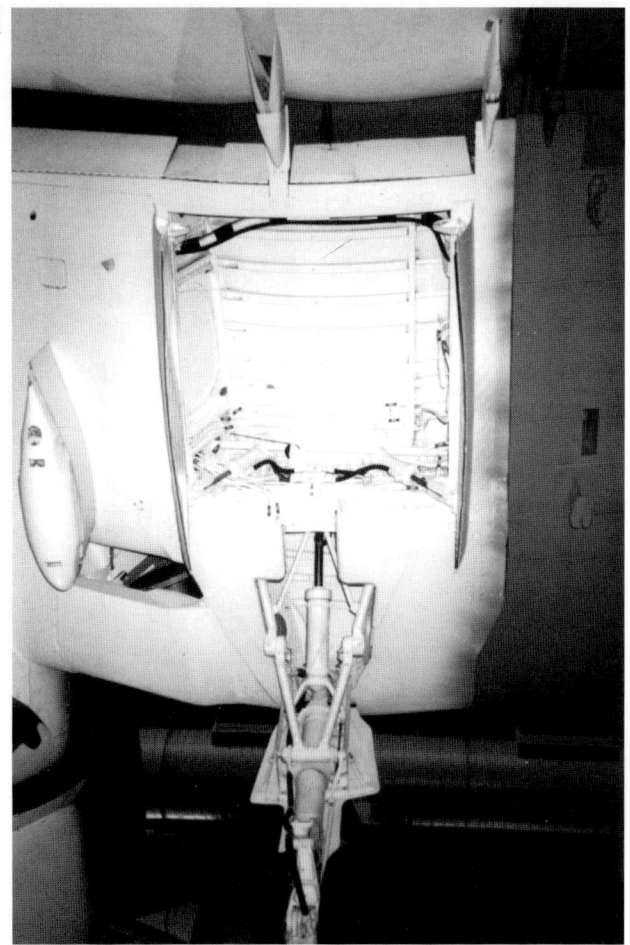

The entire right main gear well can be seen in this view. The interior of the wheel wells were often the same color as the underside of the surrounding wing, but a brownish salmon colored primer was also applied to interior surfaces on F4U-1s to include the wheel wells. It was created by mixing two ounces of Indian Red Paste in two gallons of toluol or an equivalent solvent. This mixture was then used to reduce one gallon of Zinc Chromate Primer. The resulting color would be equivalent to Federal Standard 30215. It appears to be the factory standard for F4U-1s.

The actuators that opened and closed the two side doors on the main landing gear were located at the forward end of each gear well.

This photograph looks up and aft into the right main gear well.

61

TAIL GEAR AND ARRESTING HOOK

Above, left and right: Features of the tail gear and arresting hook used on the F4U-1Ds and FG-1Ds are revealed in these two photos. The aerodynamic fairing, added just aft of the wheel slot on each gear door, was a feature found only on late FG-1Ds.

Left: This front left view shows the wheel slot and the fairing on the left tail wheel door.

Below: Details inside the tail gear well are visible in this unusual photograph. The fairings on the doors are particularly noticeable in this view.

F4U-2

The F4U-2 night fighter was not a production variant of the Corsair, because all were converted from existing F4U-1 airframes. Other publications have identified the carrier in this picture as the USS INTREPID, CV-11, because the original Navy release of the photograph provided this information in error. However, these aircraft are from VF(N)-101, and they are preparing to launch from the USS ENTERPRISE, CV-6, on a raid against Truk. The Intermediate Blue on the sides of their fuselages has been over-sprayed with black. Note the small air scoop on the side of the forward fuselage. It was for the generator which was installed in the nose section of the aircraft. The longer exhaust stubs are also visible under the cowling.
(USN via Jones)

In late 1941, before the Japanese attack on Pearl Harbor, and some seven month before the first production F4U-1 made its initial flight, the Navy expressed an interest in the development of a night fighter version of the Corsair. Although radar was still in its infancy, sets were under development that could be fitted in fighters and used for aerial intercepts at night. This was important, because on the other side of the coin, offensive systems were already being deployed that would increase the nighttime threat of reconnaissance and attack by enemy aircraft. Shortly after making its initial flight, the first production F4U-1, BuNo. 02153, was modified to become the XF4U-2 prototype.

Once the war began, the production of conventional fighters was so urgent that the Navy did not want to commit an assembly line exclusively to night fighters. Instead, thirty-two F4U-1s were designated for conversion to F4U-2 standards by the Naval Aircraft Factory in Philadelphia. Two additional aircraft would later be modified in the field by VMF(N)-532 on Roi Island.

Most noticeably, converting the F4U-1 into the F4U-2 night fighter involved the addition of an AIA radar antenna inside of a dome and fairing on the leading edge of the right wing. To make room for some equipment and help counter the weight of the radome, the outboard gun in the right wing was deleted. The pilot viewed the returns from the radar on a small scope mounted in the middle of the instrument panel. Lighting was modified, and other changes were made inside the cockpit to optimize it for night flying. A radio altimeter system and a radar beacon transponder were installed, and the standard high frequency radio was replaced with a VHF set. This eliminated the need for either of the two antenna masts usually seen on other Corsair variants. The additional electrical equipment required a more powerful generator, and to provide cooling air for it, a small scoop was installed on the right side of the forward fuselage.

Extended flame dampeners were added to the exhaust stubs, and the original short tail landing gear strut was replaced with the taller one used on F4U-1As beginning with BuNo. 50080.

VF(N)-75 became the first night fighter squadron in the Navy when it was commissioned on April 1, 1943. After training, the unit departed for the Pacific and flew its first mission on October 2, 1943. Over the next few weeks, the squadron continued to develop its night

These F4U-2s are from VMF(N)-532, and they are shown aboard the USS WINDHAM BAY, CVE-92, on July 12, 1944. The entire squadron is about to launch from the escort carrier for deployment to Saipan. Unlike the aircraft shown in the photograph at the top of this page, these F4U-2s are painted in the standard tri-color camouflage scheme. *(USN via NMNA)*

"Shirley June" was also assigned to VMF(N)-532, and it was the personal aircraft of Major Everett H. Vaughn. It is shown here on Roi Island during the second half of 1944. Note that the F4U-2s were retrofitted with the taller tail wheel assembly found on most F4U-1As and F4U-1Ds. The only antenna on the fuselage is a whip antenna just aft of the canopy. *(USN via NMNA)*

Above: A radome was added to the leading edge of the right wing to house the AIA radar. To compensate for the weight of the radome and its antenna, the outboard .50-caliber machine gun in the right wing was removed.
(Vought)

Above right: The antenna for the AIA radar was a parabolic dish which was eighteen inches in diameter.
(Vought)

Right: This view looks straight up into the radar pod and shows the electronic gear aft of the dish antenna.
(Vought)

fighting tactics, and it scored its first confirmed kill on November 1.

VF(N)-101 was the second and only other Navy squadron equipped with the F4U-2, and it also was the first to be based aboard a carrier. During the war, it operated from the USS ENTERPRISE, CV-6, and the USS ESSEX, CV-9. To help reduce visibility at night, VF(N)-101 applied black paint over the Intermediate Blue on the fuselage sides of their F4U-2s. However, they left the Intermediate Blue on the vertical tails and under the outer wing panels unchanged.

The only Marine night fighter squadron to fly the F4U-2 was VMF(N)-532 commanded by Major Everette H. Vaughn. Not only did VMF(N)-532 use their F4U-2s for night intercepts of Japanese aircraft, they also made night bombing and strafing attacks against enemy ground targets.

F4U-2s served the Navy and Marines until late 1944 when they were replaced with F6F-3N and F6F-5N night fighters with their more capable AN/APS-6 radars.

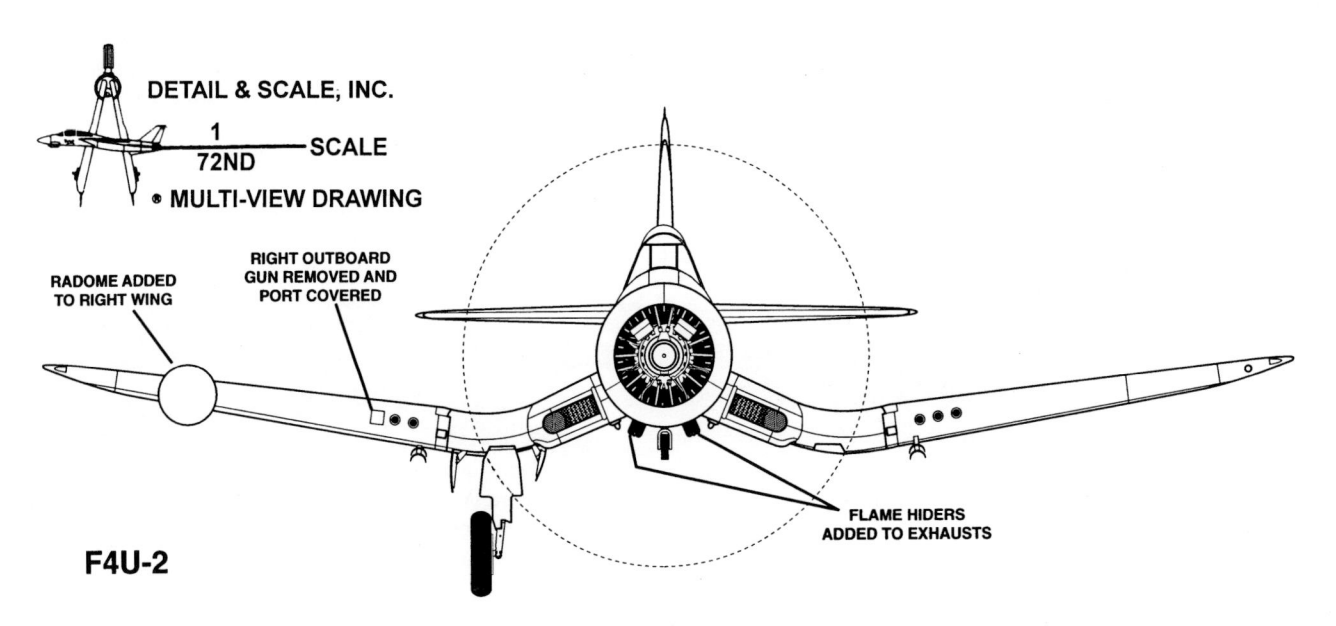

DETAIL & SCALE 1/72nd SCALE COPYRIGHT © DRAWING BY LLOYD S. JONES

DETAIL & SCALE, INC.
$\frac{1}{72ND}$ SCALE
® MULTI-VIEW DRAWING

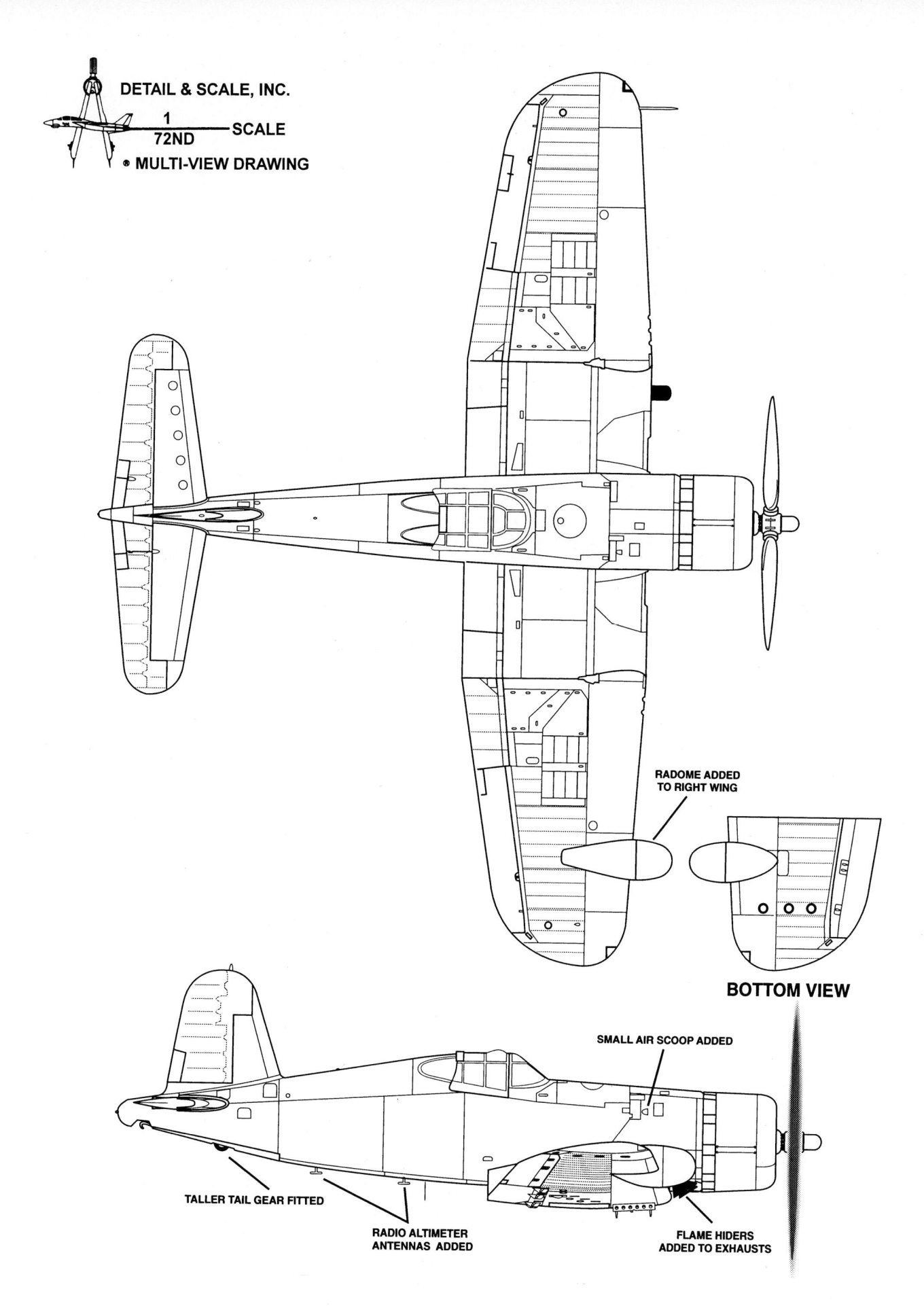

RADOME ADDED TO RIGHT WING

BOTTOM VIEW

SMALL AIR SCOOP ADDED

TALLER TAIL GEAR FITTED

RADIO ALTIMETER ANTENNAS ADDED

FLAME HIDERS ADDED TO EXHAUSTS

DETAIL & SCALE 1/72nd SCALE COPYRIGHT © DRAWINGS BY LLOYD S. JONES

XF4U-3

The three XF4U-3 prototypes were modified from existing airframes to develop a high speed, high altitude Corsair. Initial plans called for the use of a Pratt & Whitney XR-2800-16, but problems with this engine necessitated a change to the R-2800-14W This is the XF4U-3B, which was fitted with the R-2800-14W. (Vought)

The F4U-3 was to be a high speed, high altitude version of the Corsair. Plans were made for three prototypes to be converted from existing airframes to evaluate the Pratt & Whitney XR-2800-16 "C"-series engine with a Birmann turbosupercharger. The change to this powerplant necessitated the use of a four-blade Hamilton-Standard propeller.

The first prototype was called the XF4U-3A, and it was converted from F4U-1, BuNo. 17516. The turbosupercharger was installed in a large fairing under the fuselage, and the scoop was located even with the cowl flaps. This fairing was so large that it eliminated the catapult hooks, but this was of no consequence, since the proposed F4U-3 was to be used exclusively by the Marines as a land based fighter.

When developmental problems persisted with the XR-2800-16 engine, F4U-1A, BuNo. 49664, was fitted with an R-2800-14W powerplant instead, and it became the XF4U-3B. F4U-1, BuNo. 02157, was the third aircraft converted to XF4U-3 standards, but it was subsequently destroyed in a crash.

The superturbocharged engine was quite successful, and the XF4U3 could reach speeds up to 480 miles-per-hour at altitudes near 40,000 feet. But because it did not offer an appreciable increase in performance over the F4U-4, the F4U-3 never became a production variant. An order was placed for Goodyear to upgrade twenty-six FG-1Ds to XF4U-3B standards, but only thirteen of these were completed and redesignated FG-3s.

This close-up of the first XF4U-3A, BuNo. 17516, shows the large scoop for the turbosupercharger under the forward fuselage and wing center section. This aircraft had the XR-2800-16 engine installed. (Vought)

F2G

BuNo. 13471, which was one of the XF2G-1 prototype or preproduction aircraft, is shown here at Patuxent River on February 16, 1945. Note that this aircraft did not have the full bubble canopy associated with the production F2G aircraft or the heightened vertical tail with the auxiliary rudder. (USN via NMNA)

In March 1943, F4U-1, BuNo. 02460, was turned over to Pratt & Whitney so that the compatibility between the new P&W XR-4360 engine and the Corsair's airframe could be evaluated. This aircraft became known as the F4U-1WM, with the suffix letters standing for "Wasp Major," the name given to the huge twenty-eight cylinder engine. It was hoped that the 3,000 horsepower developed by the powerplant would make the Corsair a superior interceptor that could protect the fleet. Using its excellent rate of climb, a Corsair with the R-4360 engine could launch and quickly climb to an altitude in excess of 35,000 feet to intercept a Japanese reconnaissance aircraft. Likewise, it could intercept fighters, bombers, or torpedo planes that were attacking the fleet at greater distances than any of the fighters then in service.

Tests with the F4U-1WM proved successful, and the Navy assigned Goodyear the responsibility of developing production Corsair variants that were powered with the R-4360 engine. Two different versions were planned, with the F2G-1 being a land based aircraft with wings that had to be folded manually, and the F2G-2 being a carrier aircraft with hydraulically folding wings, a propeller of smaller diameter, and an arresting hook.

Seven preproduction aircraft, known as XF2G-1s, were converted from existing airframes. The first of these retained the conventional canopy and vertical tail of the

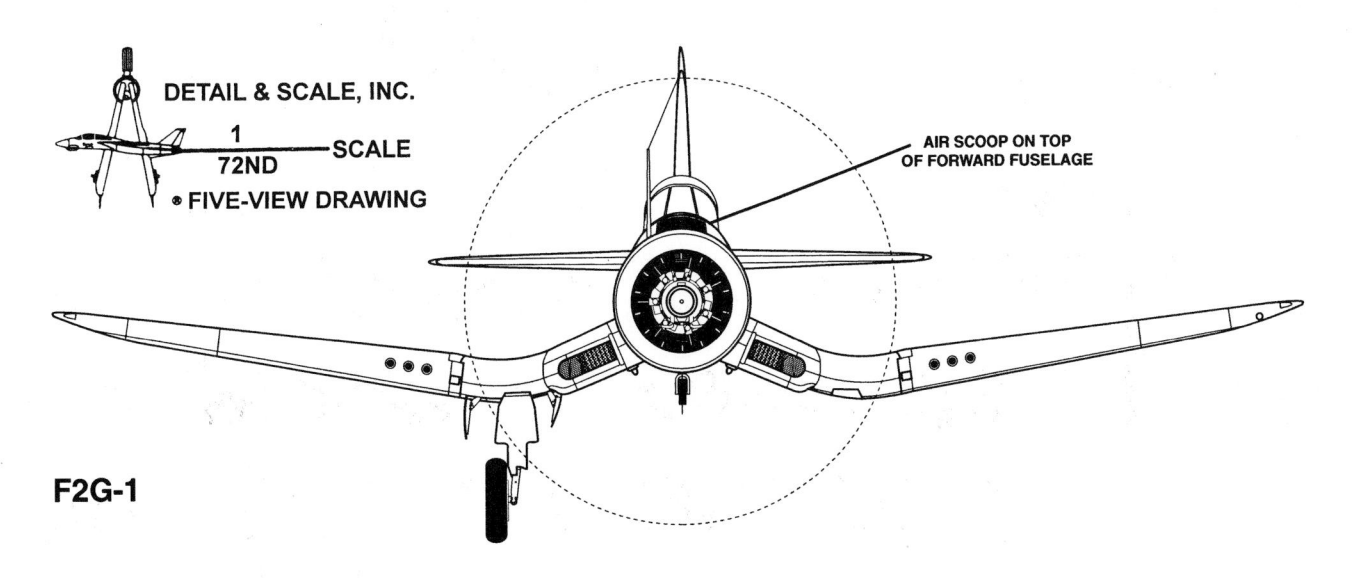

DETAIL & SCALE 1/72nd SCALE COPYRIGHT © DRAWING BY LLOYD S. JONES

67

DETAIL & SCALE, INC.
$\frac{1}{72ND}$ SCALE
• FIVE-VIEW DRAWING

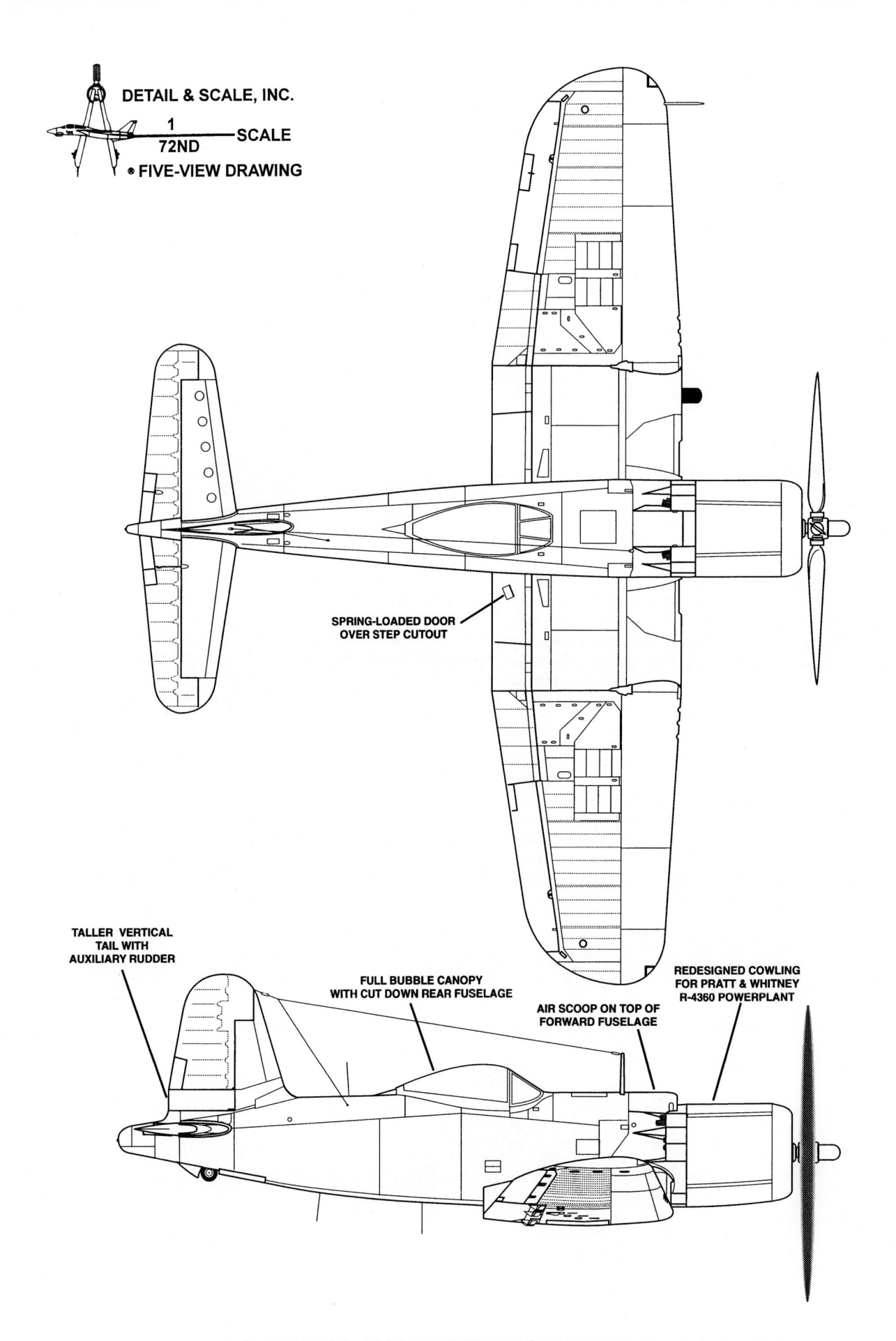

SPRING-LOADED DOOR OVER STEP CUTOUT

TALLER VERTICAL TAIL WITH AUXILIARY RUDDER

FULL BUBBLE CANOPY WITH CUT DOWN REAR FUSELAGE

AIR SCOOP ON TOP OF FORWARD FUSELAGE

REDESIGNED COWLING FOR PRATT & WHITNEY R-4360 POWERPLANT

DETAIL & SCALE 1/72nd SCALE COPYRIGHT © DRAWINGS BY LLOYD S. JONES

DETAIL & SCALE, INC.

1/72ND SCALE

® FIVE-VIEW DRAWING

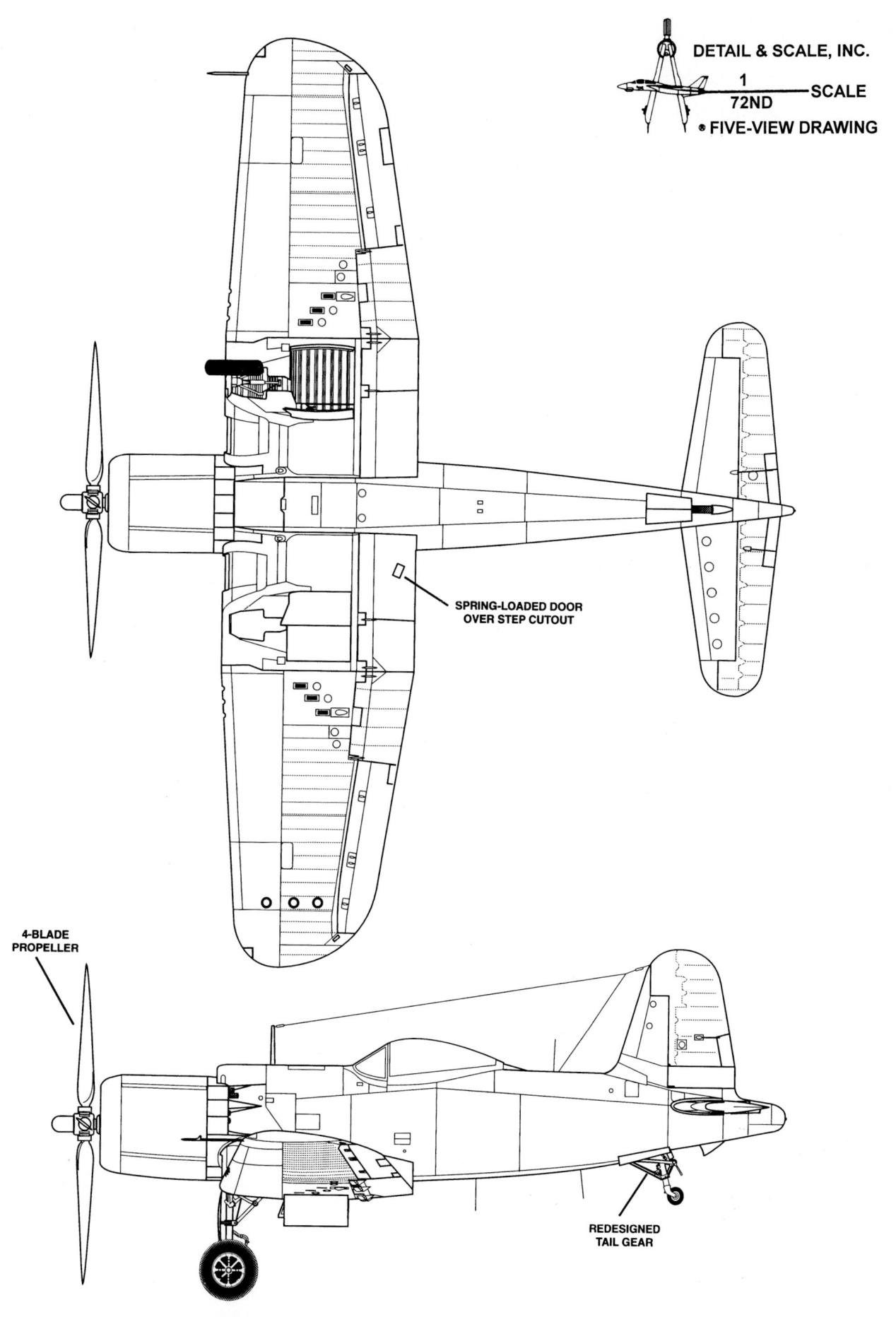

SPRING-LOADED DOOR OVER STEP CUTOUT

4-BLADE PROPELLER

REDESIGNED TAIL GEAR

DETAIL & SCALE 1/72nd SCALE COPYRIGHT © DRAWINGS BY LLOYD S. JONES

69

Another one of the XF2G-1 evaluation aircraft was BuNo. 14691. It had the full bubble canopy as seen here during a test flight in April 1945. (USN via NMNA)

BuNo. 88454 was the first of five production F2G-1 aircraft to be built. This photograph was taken while the aircraft was at the Naval Air Test Center at Patuxent River, Maryland, during testing. (USN via NMNA)

standard Corsairs, but later aircraft had a full bubble canopy and a cut down spine. The oil coolers in the wing roots had to be redesigned for the R-4360 powerplant as well. The cut out step in the inboard right flap was covered by a spring loaded door, and the cockpit was redesigned with a floor and console arrangement much like that found in the F4U-4. A large air scoop was located on the top of the forward fuselage, and several designs for this intake were evaluated.

Problems were experienced with countering the torque of the powerful engine when full power was applied during a carrier wave off and go around. Even the application of right full rudder was insufficient to turn the aircraft to the right under such conditions. This problem resulted in an unusual solution. The vertical tail was increased in height by twelve inches, and an auxiliary rudder was installed at its base. When the tail wheel was extended, the auxiliary rudder was automatically offset to the right by 12.5 degrees. Although this was not noticeable at slow speeds, when a pilot had to go to full power during a wave off, the increased airflow over the offset auxiliary rudder kept the aircraft from pulling hard to the left.

It is interesting to note that official performance figures indicate that the top speed of the F2G was only six miles per hour faster than the F4U-1D. It was even less than the F4U-4 at some altitudes. But the F2G was optimized for best rate of climb, and its initial rate of climb was 4,400 feet per minute. This was a substantial increase when compared to 3,120 feet per minute for the F4U-1D and 3,340 feet per minute for the F4U-4.

By early 1945, testing of the F2G-1s was well underway, and the kamikaze threat to ships in the Pacific had increased the urgency for the program to proceed as fast as possible. But in the next few months, dramatic changes in the war developed, and America prepared for an invasion of the Japanese homeland. Emphasis was shifted to the weapon systems that would be needed for the invasion and away from defense against the kamikaze attacks.

Perhaps more importantly, production of Grumman's F8F Bearcat was already well underway, and initial deliveries were being made to operational squadrons. These aircraft would soon be on carriers heading toward the combat zone, and the Navy believed that the F8F would be all the interceptor it needed. As a result, the contract for the F2G was reduced from over four-hundred aircraft to only five F2G-1s and five F2G-2s. Although the Navy ordered that testing should continue with these aircraft, there was never a need for further production of these Corsair variants. After being discarded by the Navy, several F2Gs became racing planes, and they participated in numerous air races for many years. One of these aircraft won the Thompson Trophy in 1947.

The Pratt & Whitney R-4360 Wasp Major powerplant could produce 3,000 horsepower, and it was the largest piston engine ever produced for use in an aircraft. It was nicknamed the "corncob" because of the appearance of its four rows of staggered cylinders.

This R-4360 is on display at the National Museum of Naval Aviation at Pensacola, Florida. Several cylinders have been removed, and the right side of the engine has been cut away to reveal some of the powerplant's internal components.

MODELERS SECTION

Note: This Modelers Section provides reviews of plastic model kits for the Corsair versions covered in this book. These include the F4U-1 through the F4U-1D. No full production kits of the XF4U-1 prototype or the F2G version had been issued by a major model company at the time this book went to press.

1/144th SCALE KITS

Mitsuwa F4U-1 Corsair

Although it is no longer generally available, this small model was issued as both a single kit and as part of a gift set which also included an F6F Hellcat.

The framed canopy indicates that it is an early F4U-1, although it comes with a centerline fuel tank and markings for an F4U-1D from the USS BUNKER HILL, CV-17. The tank looks more like one used on a Hellcat than any tank used on a Corsair, and the fit of the canopy leaves something to be desired. The area around the two rear windows is molded as part of the single-piece canopy, and care must be taken to paint the metal areas while leaving the clear windows the correct shape.

There are problems with the shape and outlines of the wings, fuselage, and tail sections, and for the most part, these will not be easy or even reasonably possible to correct. Surface detailing is in the form of very heavy panel lines which will prove difficult to correct.

Detailing is likewise not very good. There is no representation of the engine inside the cowling, and although the cockpit area is open, there is not even a seat to go in it. The intakes in the wing roots are simply flat areas on the leading edge of the wings. No antenna masts or pitot probe are provided. The propeller has a hub that is way too big, and the landing gear is not much better. It is very thick, and the doors should be replaced with ones made from thin plastic card. The holes for the guns are not molded in the wings, so these need to be drilled out.

Optional parts are provided for the landing gear so that it can be built in either the extended or retracted position, but there is no stand included if the latter choice is selected. There is an optional propeller hub with no blades to be used if a "flying" model is to be built. If the tail gear is assembled in the extended position, no gear doors are provided.

Overall, we cannot give this kit high marks, even for one in 1/144th scale. The Revell model, which is covered next, is a much better choice.

Paul Gold contributed to this review.

Revell F4U-1D

This model is clearly better than the Mitsuwa release reviewed above, and it most closely represents an early F4U-1D. It has the semi-bubble canopy with the two frames and the two pylons under the center wing section. It does not have the rockets or launch stubs, as these would be very difficult to mold in 1/144th scale. We decided to remove the wing pylons and build our review sample as an F4U-1A.

Shapes and outlines are quite good. The surface scribing is also nice and not too heavy. Although there is a trim tab located on the right aileron, this is easily removed. All other scribing is quite good for this scale.

Detailing is also better than the Mitsuwa kit. There are cylinders molded into the cowling, and while these are not a very good representation of the engine, they are better than not having anything at all. The main landing gear is much more delicate and accurate than on the Mitsuwa model. The tail gear is a bit clumsy, because Revell molded the doors and strut together as one piece. The area between the doors is solid rather than being a wheel well. It looks fine from the side, and the problem is only noticeable if you pick the model up.

The cockpit is open, but as with the Mitsuwa kit, there are no details to go inside. We added a seat and an instrument panel, and this improved the appearance of the finished model considerably. The intakes in the wing roots are open, and this looks much better than the flat areas on the Mitsuwa kit.

The canopy is a bit thick, and it is oversized. It will not fit well on the finished fuselage, and there isn't much that can be done about this problem. There are no antenna masts, and the pitot probe is likewise not included. We easily made these from sprue. The gun ports are not molded in the wing, so these must carefully be drilled out.

For the most part, this is a pretty good kit as 1/144th scale fighters go. Like the Mitsuwa kit, it is no longer generally available, but it is not too difficult to find one at swap meets.

The Mitsuwa 1/144th scale model of the F4U-1 is no longer in production and is very difficult to find. Paul Gold built this model straight from the box and used the kit decals. However, they are markings for an F4U-1D aboard the USS BUNKER HILL, CV-17, so they are incorrect for an F4U-1 which the kit represents. (Gold)

Revell's 1/144th scale Corsair is also out of production, but it is the better of the two 1/144th scale Corsairs that have been produced. The author built this model to represent an F4U-1A from VMF-215. It was flown by 1Lt. Robert M. Hanson at Torokina in February 1944.

1/72nd SCALE KITS

Airfix/MPC/Heller F4U-1D

Originally released by Airfix, then by MPC, this kit has also been sold under the Heller label. However, it should not be confused with the original Heller Corsair reviewed below. They are two completely different models.

The parts most closely represent an early F4U-1D. The pylons are present under the center wing section, but it has the semi-bubble canopy with the frames, and there are no rocket launchers present under the outer wing sections. It is covered with rivets and has very little in the way of panel lines. The cowling is completely devoid of detail, and not even the cowl flaps are represented.

The old Airfix kit was covered by rivets and it was not well detailed. Jim Roeder of Salinas, California, finished this model with markings from VMF-511 and the second USS BLOCK ISLAND, CVE-106. (Roeder)

Detailing is almost non-existent. A series of raised lines inside the cowling are supposed to be the rods and cylinders on the engine, and the crankcase is a featureless rounded cylinder at its center. The cockpit has only a crude seat and pilot, and even the area above the instrument panel is missing. This is very noticeable, even under the closed, single-piece canopy and windscreen.

The landing gear isn't any better. It lacks detailing, and the wells are open and featureless. The main struts are too thin and too long, and the retraction arms are one thin rod which do not touch the top of the wells. The tail gear doors do not have the slots in them, and the tail gear strut does not come close to being an accurate representation of the real thing. Shapes for all of the main gear doors are likewise inaccurate. The wheels are quite concave, rather than being generally flat like they should be.

The two pylons are molded as part of the wings, and they are incorrect in shape. Two bombs are provided to go on them, and they too leave something to be desired where accuracy is concerned. There are no antenna masts included, but most F4U-1Ds had at least one.

In short, this is not an accurate kit, and with far better models of the Corsair available in 1/72nd scale, this one is best left to the collectors or to children who are just learning to model.

Jim Roeder contributed to this review.

Hasegawa F4U-1

Although the three Hasegawa kits are the best "dash one" series Corsair models in 1/72nd scale, they still leave much to be desired. We will begin by giving a full review for the F4U-1, then follow by explaining the differences in the F4U-1D and F4U-2 releases.

The F4U-1 kit comes close to representing the basic features of the real aircraft, except that the inboard flap on the right wing has the cut out step in it. This did not become a standard feature until well into the F4U-1D production run, and while some F4U-1s may have had a flap with the step installed as a replacement, it would be rare and well after this early version of the Corsair had been relegated to training roles. The kit also comes with a centerline fuel tank, and the provision for these tanks was not a standard feature until F4U-1A production.

Surface scribing is very fine, but it is incomplete and inaccurate. The trim tab is missing from the left aileron, and the noticeable round access panels on the top of the left horizontal stabilizer and the bottom of the right horizontal stabilizer are also missing. The scribing for the gun bay covers are likewise incomplete and not entirely accurate. The steps in the top of each wing, which are covered by spring-loaded doors, are missing as is the covered step in the right side of the fuselage. The hand holds are not present on each side of the fuselage, nor is the fuel tank filler on top of the forward fuselage. The three identification lights under the right wing tip, the blue formation light on top of each wing tip, and the white recognition light on top of the right wing are all missing. The fillers for each of the outer wing tanks are likewise missing, as are the drains for these tanks beneath the wings. In short, more of the F4U-1's features are not included in the scribing than those that are.

Curiously, the outer flap on each wing is represented as being fabric covered, however, all flaps were skinned with metal. The ailerons, which were made of plywood and covered with fabric, have no fabric representation. The simulation of the fabric covering on the outer wing panels, elevators, and rudder is nicely done.

The engine is rather poorly detailed, and only the forward row of cylinders is fully represented. Noticeable details on the crankcase are missing, and the housing itself is too long. This causes the engine to sit too far aft in the cowling. While the kit engine may be acceptable to some modelers, better after-market R-2800 engines are available in 1/72nd scale, and these will make a considerable improvement in the model's appearance.

This Hasegawa 1/72nd scale F4U-1 was built by J. C. Bahr. It represents an aircraft from VMF-214 which was flown by Lt. Edwin L. Olander and named "Marines's Dream." (Liles)

The cockpit is totally wrong. It has a floor and side consoles like that found in the F4U-4 and later variants. We strongly recommend using the inexpensive True Details cockpit detailing set designed for the Hasegawa 1/72nd scale Corsairs. It represents the floorless cockpit very well, and it looks good inside the completed model.

The canopy and windscreen are molded together, and the two rear windows are separate pieces. The framed canopy is the later type with the blister for the rear view mirror. These are all quite adequate, but Squadron has a set of vacu-formed clear canopies for this kit which look more in scale. Using the Squadron canopies also makes it simple to display the canopy in the open position.

The landing gear detail is adequate, but the two retraction arms on each main gear are represented by a single wide bar. This is reasonable in 1/72nd scale, but the appearance can be improved by cutting it off and rebuilding it with thin plastic strips. The wheel wells are too shallow, but this again is reasonable considering the scale thickness of the plastic. The wheels and tires are quite good, and the main tires have a diamond tread on them. All main gear doors have nice detailing on their inside surfaces. The tail gear is the original short type which is correct for the F4U-1 variant.

Fit is generally good except where the aft end of the lower fuselage on the wing assembly fits on to the completed fuselage. The fit of the engine inside the cowling is critical, because the forward fuselage actually assembles to the back of the engine. We recommend thinning the inside of the cowl flaps to a scale thickness before gluing the cowl assembly in place.

Until a better 1/72nd scale Corsair kit is released, the Hasegawa models are the ones to use. But the modeler must scribe in a number of important features that Hasegawa failed to include. The cockpit must be replaced, and some modelers will want to replace the engine. If all of this is done, the resulting model will be a very good replica of the real thing.

J. C. Bahr and Jim Roeder contributed to this review.

Hasegawa F4U-1D

The box art claims that this model is an F4U-1D, but the plastic inside comes closest to being an early F4U-1A prior to the heightening of the tail gear. Hasegawa failed to change the tail gear to the taller type used on most F4U-1As. The step in the inboard right flap is again present, and this is incorrect for F4U-1As and many F4U-1Ds.

This release also has neither the wing pylons, found on all F4U-1Ds, or the rocket stubs installed on most of them. Anyone wanting to build an F4U-1D or FG-1D from this kit will have to add the wing pylons in all cases and the rocket stubs for most aircraft. The canopy is the clear-vision type without the two top braces, and this indicates a late F4U-1D. It is a simple matter to paint these braces on if they are appropriate for the aircraft being modeled. Here again, Squadron has excellent vacu-formed thin canopies which look more in scale and which can be easily displayed in the open position.

The two fuselage halves were changed to accept the semi-bubble canopy, otherwise, all parts are exactly the same as they were for the F4U-1 issue.

J. C. Bahr and Jim Roeder contributed to this review.

Hasegawa F4U-2

To create the F4U-2 night fighter, Hasegawa began with their F4U-1 model and added most of the required parts. These included a two-piece radome, six extensions for the exhaust stubs with two bases for them, a plug for the outer right side gun, and the small scoop for the forward right side of the fuselage. However, Hasegawa failed to include the taller tail gear that was fitted to these night fighter conversions.

In building our review sample, we used the new ProModeler instrument panel decals for U. S. Navy and Marine World War II fighters (sheet 88-1011). These unique decals are accurate right down to the sub-variant, and they have clear over each instrument to simulate glass. Both complete panels and individual instruments are provided, as are seat belts and shoulder harnesses.

Hasegawa's F4U-2 in 1/72nd scale was used by the author to build this Corsair night fighter from VF(N)-101.

Walt Fink used the Hasegawa 1/72nd scale F4U-1D release to build this model of a Corsair from VMF-351 when that unit operated from the USS CAPE GLOUCESTER, CVE-109. (Fink)

Hawk/Testors F4U-1D

This very crude kit was first issued by Hawk in the 1950s, and many different releases followed. It later became a Testors kit when that company took over the now defunct Hawk line. In every case, it is very inaccurate and has almost no detailing.

The engine is molded into the very end of the cowling and takes the form of primitive cylinders. The crankcase is almost non-existent. The cockpit is completely closed over and does not even have a pilot's head in it. There are five bogus pylons under each outer wing panel, and eight very crude rockets and two bombs are included to go on them. A centerline fuel tank is also provided, and perhaps this is the only part of the model that is usable.

The landing gear is both simplistic and inaccurate, and none of the gear doors have the correct shape. Surface scribing is a mix of recessed and raised panel lines which are generally incorrect and far from being complete. In short, this model is not one that could be considered by the serious scale modeler.

Jim Roeder contributed to this review.

Heller (Aurora) F4U

This kit actually traces its origins back to Aurora, but it was in the Heller line far longer. It should not be confused with the present Heller Corsair I kit which is the old Airfix model reboxed under the Heller label.

With no under-wing pylons or rocket launchers, the model most closely represents an F4U-1A. The panel lines are raised, while the control surfaces are outlined with recessed lines. Although incomplete, what is there is fairly accurate with a few exceptions. This is the only F4U-1 series model in 1/72nd scale that includes the fillers for the outer wing tanks in the scribing. The three identification lights under the right wing tip are also represented, but the middle one is too far forward. The right aileron has a trim tab, and it should only have the balance tab at its inboard end. The lights on top of the wings are all missing, as are the very noticeable actuators for the trim and balance tabs on the elevators. The round access panels are scribed into the tops of both horizontal stabilizers, but they should be on the top of the left and the bottom of the right stabilizer.

The engine is very crude and has cone shaped cylinders with no details. The crankcase does have representations of the magnetos, but they are not the correct shape. An after-market engine is strongly recommended for anyone building this model.

A cockpit interior is provided, but it is totally incorrect. Most noticeably, it has the cockpit floor which is inaccurate for any "dash one" Corsair. The True Details cockpit set for the Hasegawa kits will fit and should be substituted. The windscreen and canopy are in two pieces and can be displayed opened or closed. The canopy is the semi-bubble design with the two overhead frames as used on F4U-1As and early F4U-1Ds.

The wings are designed to be built in the extended or folded position. We recommend sticking with the extended option, because there is nothing in the way of detailing for the fold area. Regardless of how the wings are assembled, the fit is very poor, and much filling and sanding will be required.

The landing gear is adequate, but it could be improved. Only single retraction arms are provided for the main gear struts, and they do not reach to their locating holes inside the wheel wells. The main wheels are ac-

The original Heller 1/72nd scale kit was used by Jim Roeder to build this model of "Pappy" Boyington's F4U-1A named "Lulabelle." (Roeder)

ceptable for the outside, but the inside of each wheel lacks detailing. The tires are the smooth type with no tread on them. We recommend using True Detail resin wheels and tires available in set 72025. The wheel wells also lack detailing and are not completely enclosed. Detailing on the inside of the main gear doors is present, but it is both inaccurate and inconsistent. For the tail gear, the kit provides the original short type which was used on F4U-1 and early F4U-1As. For most Corsairs that can be represented by this kit, the strut will have to be lengthened to make it the correct height for the later design. The tail wheel doors are separate parts, and while they do have the slots in them, there is no detailing on the inside surfaces.

With work, this kit can be built into a decent model, but the Hasegawa and Jo Han kits are better, and we recommend using one of them instead.

Jim Roeder contributed to this review.

Jo Han F4U-1

Although the box art says this is an F4U-1 Corsair, it comes closer to representing an F4U-1D than any other 1/72nd scale kit available today. While they are not accurate in shape, the pylons are molded under the center wing section. Eight rockets and launch stubs are included to go under the outer wing panels, and the canopy is the semi-bubble design with the two frames near the top. However, the tail gear is the early short type, and this is incorrect for the F4U-1D or FG-1D. It will have to be lengthened except for some very early F4U-1As. Overall, it is not as good as the Hasegawa models, but it does have some features that are better than those found in the Hasegawa kits.

Surface scribing is recessed, and it is a little heavy. A number of important features are missing or not correctly represented. The circular access panels are on top of both horizontal tails, rather than being on top of the left and the bottom of the right. But the representation of the trim and balance tabs on the elevators and their actuators are better than on any other 1/72nd scale "dash one" series Corsair. There are no identification, forma-

Jim Roeder used the Jo Han 1/72nd scale kit to build a model of Ira Kepford's famous number 29.

tion, or recognition lights scribed into the wing surfaces. Only the navigation lights on the leading edge of each tip have been represented. The step on the right side of the fuselage and the hand holds are likewise missing.

The strong point of the model is its engine. It is clearly the best in any 1/72nd scale Corsair model, and it has both rows of cylinders. The magnetos are present on the crankcase, but they need to be reshaped a bit to have the correct cylindrical design when viewed from the top.

At the other end of the spectrum, the cockpit is non-existent. Only an L-shaped seat is present, and not even the area under the windscreen is represented. This results in a large hole being left under the windscreen and canopy when the model is finished. Here again, the True Details cockpit detailing set 72453 will prove helpful.

Two decent 500-pound bombs are provided for the pylons, and the rockets are molded with their launch stubs in place. The fins are molded as a + when viewed from behind, but they should be an X. Simply cut the fins off each rocket and rotate them forty-five degrees to obtain the correct appearance.

The landing gear is overly simplistic, and it does not accurately represent the real thing. The wheel wells are open, and they are devoid of any detailing. The gear doors are generally the correct shape, but they are too thick and have no detailing on their inner surfaces. The main gear wheels should be replaced with resin ones available from True Details in wheel set 72025.

The interior parts for the oil cooler intakes are very inaccurate, and new ones need to be made from scrap plastic. The centerline fuel tank is quite good, and two antenna masts and a decent pitot probe are provided. The canopy and windscreen are molded as a single piece which is clear and quite accurate. It has a good fit when it is glued to the fuselage.

If the True Details cockpit is added, and the area above the instrument panel is made from scratch, this kit can be used to build a good model of the F4U-1A or F4U-1D. Some additional features need to be scribed into the skin of the aircraft, and the landing gear wells should be closed in and detailed. Some reworking of the gear struts would also help, but all of this is relatively simple if the modeler wants to put the time into it. We believe this model is worth considering, although the Hasegawa kits would still be the better choice.

Jim Roeder contributed to this review.

Revell F4U-1D

When this kit was released over thirty years ago, it was easily the best 1/72nd scale Corsair on the market. But the years have taken their toll, and in spite of the problems with the Hasegawa kit, it is better than this one from Revell.

The box says the model is of an F4U-1D, and the pylons under the center wing section are provided. However, there are no fuel tanks or bombs to go on them. There also are no rocket launchers or rockets for the outer wing panels, and the tail gear has the short strut which is not correct for an F4U-1D. The canopy is the semi-bubble design with the overhead braces as found on the F4U-1A and early F4U-1Ds. It is therefore much easier to simply delete the pylons and build the kit as an F4U-1A.

Surface detailing is in the form of fine raised lines, but it is incomplete and not always accurate. The same is true for the recessed lines which represent the outlines of the control surfaces. The right aileron has a trim tab, which it shouldn't, and only single tabs are represented on each elevator instead of two.

The engine is oversimplified and consists of conical cylinders which are devoid of detail. The crankcase is too small and short, and it has no representation of the magnetos or other details that should be there.

As with other 1/72nd scale Corsair models, this one has a floor in the cockpit which is not correct. A crude seat is molded on the floor, and a pilot figure is provided. No instrument panel, control column, or other detailing parts are included for the cockpit. The canopy and windscreen are separate parts, and the canopy may be displayed in the open position. Both the windscreen and canopy are too wide and present a flat appearance.

The landing gear is crude, simplistic, and poorly molded. There is no detailing on the doors, and the tires are simply small donuts. Detailing on the wheels is also inaccurate and incomplete. The instructions show the forward landing gear doors upside down.

All things considered, this is not a very good model, and it is best left to the collectors.

The author used the old Revell 1/72nd scale kit to build this model of a Corsair flown by Marine Captain Philip C. DeLong of VMF-212.

SMER F4U-1

This is a reissue of the Heller kit reviewed above. The only difference is that it has a small tree of etched metal parts for detailing the cockpit and the landing gear. These parts are not really accurate, and most importantly, they do not get rid of the floor in the cockpit which is incorrect for this Corsair variant.

1/48th SCALE KITS

AMT F4U-1

From the propeller to the horizontal stabilizer, this kit is very inaccurate and lacks detailing. It was the first birdcage Corsair model on the market, but when released, modelers soon realized there was not much they could do with it to try to make it look like the real thing. Even the one-piece canopy is wrong. On each side, the rear piece of glass should not have any framework on its trailing edge, but these pieces of glass are not even represented. The indentions in the fuselage halves for the two side windows are way too shallow, and no glass is provided for them.

Major items are missing. There is no representation for the guns in the wings. There are no holes where the blast tubes would be, no shell ejector slots, and no scribing for the gun bay access doors. Likewise, no pitot probe or antenna masts are provided.

What is included in the kit is inaccurate. The cockpit has a floor, and the instrument panel is completely incorrect. All of the landing gear doors are the wrong shape, and the wheels have spokes on both sides. The cowl flaps are represented by evenly spaced lines etched into the plastic, but the real flaps were not all the same size.

There is simply nothing to say positive about this kit that would justify its use as a scale model. Fortunately, much better 1/48th scale models of the F4U-1 have been released by other model manufacturers.

Dave Pluth used the old AMT 1/48th scale F4U-1 to build a model of an early Corsair that served on Guadalcanal with VMF-213. This kit lacks even basic detailing, and it has numerous inaccuracies. (Pluth)

Hobbycraft F4U-1

Molded in light gray plastic, this kit has nicely executed engraved panel lines that are generally accurate. But a few problems do exist. The white recognition light on top of the right wing is missing. The right aileron has a trim tab, and it shouldn't. Both horizontal stabilizers have the round access panels on the top, but the ones on the right stabilizer should be on the bottom. The biggest problem with the surface detailing is clearly the total lack of any representation of the very noticeable trim and balance tabs on each of the elevators. These must be scribed into the plastic, and thin stretched sprue or very fine wire should be added to represent the actuators. The window is provided for the lower fuselage, but it is the incorrect shape, being too tapered at the rear.

The engine looks fine until it is installed inside the cowling, then it becomes obvious that the crankcase is too long. Another problem in this area is that the opening in the front of the cowling is too small. The cowl flaps can be built open or closed, but either way fit is poor. The top flaps were usually sealed in a closed position to prevent oil from blowing back onto the windscreen.

There are a number of fit problems in this kit, and the wings are no exception. The oil coolers are difficult to install correctly, and the flaps are worse. To assemble them in the lowered position, it is necessary to remove the bumps under the wings where they fit. But Hobbycraft also did not provide the spanners that go between the inner and center flaps when they are extended, and this omission is very noticeable. It will be necessary to make them from plastic card. While working on the wings, drill out the blast tubes for the guns to give them more depth and make them slightly larger.

There are fit problems with the fuselage as well. The turtledeck plug that goes just behind the cockpit is too small, and the best thing to do is even the amount that must be filled and sanded on each side.

Cockpit detail is not up to the standards found in many of today's 1/48th scale kits, and it has a floor with

Hobbycraft's 1/48th scale F4U-1 was used by Mac Cailein Mor to build this model of an early Corsair flown by 2Lt. Kenneth Walsh, the first Corsair pilot to become an ace and the first to receive the Medal of Honor.

a hole in it. This is a poor attempt to represent the true floorless cockpit of these early Corsairs. But the birdcage canopy is very well executed and looks good on the finished model. True Details Cockpit Set 48460 is designed for the Hobbycraft Corsairs, and we recommend using it to replace what comes in the kit.

The landing gear is quite acceptable for a 1/48th scale model, and both short and tall options are provided for the tail gear.

Although it is considerably better than the AMT kit, it is not in the same class as the Tamiya F4U-1 reviewed below. But the Tamiya kit is much more expensive, and it will be up to the individual modeler to decide if he is willing to pay the extra amount for the additional quality.

Hobbycraft F4U-2 Night Fighter

This kit is the same as the one above, except that extra parts are provided to build the F4U-2 night fighter. These include a two-piece radome, a different arrangement for the guns in the right wings where the outboard blast tube is removed, and the flash hiders for the exhausts. The part for the guns in the right wing simply has the outer hole eliminated instead of having the correct cover for it, and the flash hiders for the exhausts are very poorly represented. The small scoop for the right side of the forward fuselage was not included, but this was a feature on all F4U-2s. Also missing are the radio altimeter antennas that go under the aft fuselage, and these should be provided in 1/48th scale.

Hobbycraft F4U-1A

This kit is the same as the F4U-1 model covered above, but it has a different plug for the turtledeck as well as the windscreen and clear-vision canopy found on all but early F4U-1Ds. It is a simple matter to paint the two overhead frames on the canopy if they are appropriate for the particular Corsair being modeled.

A Brewster bomb rack and a bomb are provided for the centerline station, and an external fuel tank is also included as an option. The two pylons that were mounted under the wing's center section on F4U-1Ds are also provided, so there is a possibility of building a -1D. However, there are no rockets or launch stubs, so these must be obtained from another kit. Otherwise, all comments in the review of the Hobbycraft F4U-1 above apply to this kit as well.

Hobbycraft F4U-1D

This issue is the same as the F4U-1A model reviewed above, but it has a choice of bombs, fuel tanks, or finned napalm tanks to go on the two pylons under the center wing section. If the modeler wants to represent external fuel tanks, we recommend using the napalm tanks without the fins rather than the fuel tanks that are provided. Unfortunately, no rockets or launch rails are included with this issue, and most F4U-1Ds had this provision.

Hobbycraft FG-1D

Hobbycraft calls this issue a COIN (counter-insurgency) version of the Corsair. It is the same as the F4U-1D model reviewed above, except that this release has eight five-inch rockets and their launch rails instead of the bombs, fuel tanks, and napalm tanks of the F4U-1D issue.

But curiously, no stores are provided for the two pylons that go under the center section of the wing. Also included in this kit are two ADF "football" antennas.

Dave Pluth and Stan Parker contributed to the reviews of the Hobbycraft kits.

Otaki/Arii F4U-1A

Released first by Otaki, this was the best Corsair model on the market for many years. It still compares favorably with other 1/48th scale Corsairs.

The propeller is nicely done, but for some reason, there are indented ovals on the front of each blade where the Hamilton-Standard logo decals should go. Fill these in with putty and sand them smooth. The engine has a crankcase that is too squashed in appearance, and the magnetos are not very accurate. Only the front row of cylinders are represented, so it would be best to find a better R-2800 from another kit or use one from an aftermarket source. Arii releases have a mold flaw on the cowling, but this is not found on most Otaki kits.

The cockpit is completely wrong. The instrument panel is inaccurate, and there is a floor beneath the seat. AeroMaster once made a super detailing set for this kit, but it is no longer generally available. If one can be found, it is highly recommended, and if not, it might be possible to make some adjustments and do some trimming in order to use the True Details cockpit detail set that was designed for the Hobbycraft kits.

The landing gear is adequate, although the main tires are the treadless type and the tail wheel needs some detailing. True Details makes a nice resin set of tires for the Hellcat and Corsair in 1/48th scale, and we recommend using these instead. These are True Details stock number 48045. Only the tall tail strut design is provided, and it was found on most F4U-1As and all F4U-1Ds.

The only external store that is provided is a centerline fuel tank. Surface detailing is well executed and very accurate in most respects. The actuating arms for all of the elevator tabs are the same, and this is incorrect. The one for the tab on the rudder is located too high. Also, the outer flap on each wing is represented as being fabric covered, but the real thing was skinned with metal. The

An F4U-1D from the USS BUNKER HILL, CV-17, was chosen by the author as the subject for this Otaki model in 1/48th scale.

tab arrangement on both ailerons is correct, and all identification lights are represented. The white recognition light on the top of the right wing is not present, but it was deleted from most F4U-1As during production. The exhausts are simply engraved into the lower fuselage, and they would have looked much better if they had been separate pieces.

With a new engine and cockpit interior, this is still a good kit, and an excellent model can be built from it with a moderate amount of effort. It fits together well, and requires little filling and sanding.

Dave Pluth contributed to this review.

Tamiya F4U-1 & F4U-2

Without a doubt, this is the best Corsair model on the market, and it is difficult to fault it. The few goofs are rather minor and relatively easy to correct. The filler caps for the leading edge wing tanks are located too far outboard. They should be just inboard of the third panel line in from each wing tip, not the second. Simply fill them in and scribe new ones in the correct locations. The white position light on the top of the right wing is missing, and this was on all F4U-1, FG-1, and F3A-1 Corsairs. The cut out step in the inner right flap is present, and this did not become a standard feature until well into the production run of F4U-1Ds. It should be filled in with plastic card, then filled with modeling putty and sanded smooth.

A Brewster bomb rack and bomb are included for the centerline station, but Navy records indicate that provisions for these were not standard until production of the F4U-1A. Similar makeshift racks, which were installed in the field, were fitted to a few of the F4U-1 Corsairs, however. An external fuel tank is provided as an optional centerline store, but here again, records indicate that F4U-1s did not have standard provisions for the use of these tanks. Perhaps Tamiya intended these parts to be used on future releases, but they are shown on the instruction sheet in this kit. Use them with caution and only if photographic evidence confirms that they are correct for the specific aircraft being modeled.

Otherwise, the model is superior in every respect, and it is the kit by which all other Corsair models must be judged. It is quite expensive, but there is no need for any after-market parts.

The R-2800 engine comes in four pieces, and it is as well detailed and as accurate as many of the specialized resin engines that are available from after-market sources. The cowl flaps are separate and can be built in the open or closed position.

The wings are detailed with recessed panel lines and some raised details. There are several options available as the wings are assembled. These include all the parts necessary to complete the wing structure in the extended or folded position. If built in the folded position, the hinge area on both the center and outer sections is very well detailed, and the braces that extend from the fuselage to the wing are included in the kit. Likewise, the flaps may be assembled extended or retracted, and in all cases, fit is excellent. Unlike the Hobbycraft kit, the gap filler between the inner and center flaps on each wing is present. The design and engineering of the wing assembly is well

Tamiya's excellent 1/48th scale F4U-1 was used by Dave Pluth of Chaska, Minnesota, to build this model of a Corsair flown by Lt(jg) James Halford of VF-17. (Pluth)

thought out and very sturdy.

The cockpit is a real jewel, and it is essentially a model in and of itself. It is the correct floorless design, and all details are well represented. A decal is provided for the instrument panel, but we recommend using the ProModeler 1/48th scale decal sheet 88-1021 which has Hellcat and Corsair instrument panels and individual instruments on it. By using the individual instrument decals, the details of each instrument will be accurately represented, and the finished instrument will appear to have glass over it. The kit also provides a decal for the seat belts.

Below the cockpit, the bomb aiming window is provided to go in the lower fuselage. Unlike the one in the Hobbycraft kit, it is the correct size and shape. Both of the framed canopy designs are included as options. One is the original flat version, and the other has the blister for the rear view mirror. In either case, they may be assembled in the opened or the closed position. Other clear parts include the two rear side windows, the windscreen, the gun sight, the armored glass beneath the windscreen, and the landing/taxi light under the left wing.

Detailing in the wheel wells is excellent, and all of the doors are the correct shape and also have accurate details. The landing gear is superb, and all of the retraction and support arms are present. The oleos are the correct length, which is something that is lacking in many other Corsair kits. The main tires have the rib style tread on them, and both long and short tail wheel struts are provided. For the F4U-1, the short strut should be used.

Verlinden produced a super detailing set for this kit, and with it, the model can be turned into a real masterpiece. But almost all modelers will be quite satisfied with the super amount of detailing that comes in the kit itself.

Fit is generally excellent throughout. Some filling and sanding will be required around the fuselage plug that goes just aft of the cockpit.

Optional parts are also provided to build an F4U-2 night fighter. These include a two-piece radome, the extended exhaust stubs, a cover for the right outboard gun, the small scoop on the forward right fuselage, and two radio altimeter antennas under the aft fuselage. Be sure to use the taller tail gear strut if building the F4U-2.

Anyone who studies the way this kit was designed can easily tell that Tamiya plans other versions in later releases. For example, holes that will be opened up in the center wing section for the pylons used on the F4U-1D are present, although there are none for the rocket rails. The use of the plug behind the cockpit is another indication of future versions to come. When they become available, they will undoubtedly be the best Corsair models of each subsequent variant that is released.

Dave Pluth and Jim Roeder contributed to this review.

1/32nd SCALE KIT

Revell F4U-1A

The only plastic model kit of a Corsair in 1/32nd scale was first released by Revell in 1970. It has been issued several times since, but in each case, only the box art, instructions, and decals have changed. In the Smithsonian National Air and Space Museum Collection release, the box art claims that the model is an F4U-1D, but the plastic has always represented an F4U-1A. It does not have the pylons that go under the center wing section or the launch stubs or rockets for the outer wing panels. The tail gear strut is the early short design used on F4U-1s and early F4U-1As. However, it is a simple matter to change this to the taller strut with the use of a plastic rod. The windscreen and canopy are two separate pieces that can be displayed in the opened or closed positions, and the canopy is the semi-bubble type with the two braces at the top.

The shape and outline of the kit are generally good, and surface detailing is in the form of raised panel lines. For some reason, Revell also used raised lines to represent the flaps, and this is very poor. They will have to be rescribed if they are to look right. However, the ailerons, elevators, and rudder are all outlined with nice recessed lines. Some features on the surface are missing, and these include the three identification lights under the right wing, the formation lights on top of the wings, and the white recognition light that goes on top of the right wing tip. This last item would only be on F4U-1s and early F4U-1As. There is no representation of the filler caps for the two leading edge wing tanks, and a number of panel lines are also missing. The spoiler that was located on the leading edge of the right wing on F4U-1As and later versions is likewise not included.

The actuators for the tabs on the elevators are incorrect, but the Eduard detailing set has the long actuators for the elevator tabs. There is what appears to be an actuator for the rudder's trim tab on the right side, but the actuator should only be on the left. The step on the right side of the fuselage is open, but on the actual aircraft it would be covered by a spring loaded door. The cut out step in the right inboard flap is also open. This step did not become standard until well into the production of the F4U-1D/FG-1D variant. The hand holds on either side of the windscreen are missing and need to be scribed in place.

The engine assembly consists of eight parts, but it needs some detailing in the form of wires and other small items. Because they were molded as part of the crank-

The only Corsair kit in 1/32nd scale is this old model from Revell. It lacks detailing, and several inaccuracies should be corrected. The author built this model straight out of the box over twenty-five years ago, and it represents an F4U-1A flown by Major George L. Hollowell of VMF-111.

case, the magnetos are not the correct cylindrical shape, and they should be reworked. But with a little time and effort, the engine can be made to look very realistic.

Detailing in the cockpit is very incomplete and inaccurate. A floor is provided, and it is not correct for any Corsair up through the F4U-1D. Eduard makes a detailing set that will be helpful, and we recommend its use. As this book was being written, Lone Star Models was almost finished with a resin detailing set for the cockpit interior that also provided main wheels and tires. Several other sets were also being developed. These included a resin flap set and a wheel well set that included new landing gear doors. Conversion kits were under development for the F4U-1, F4U-5, and F2G. Each of these had the appropriate canopy as well as resin parts. For modelers who are interested in any of these detailing or conversion kits, we recommend writing to Lone Star Models at 13758 Drakewood, Sugar Land, Texas 77478.

A feature of the kit is an operating wing fold. The hinge area is not well detailed, and what is there is not very accurate. The simplest thing to do is build the model with the wings extended, but an ambitious modeler could do a lot of detailing and make the wing fold look realistic.

The biggest problem with the landing gear is that the wheel wells are all open and have no detailing. This is very noticeable on such a large model, so a lot of work must be done in this area as well. The struts and wheels are over-simplified, and they too will need some help. The Eduard detailing set has some etched metal parts that will improve the appearance of the landing gear struts. But the wheels are inaccurate and the tires are smooth and featureless. We recommend using the Lone Star Models' wheels instead. The gear doors are generally the correct shape, but they are devoid of any detailing on their inside surfaces. Lone Star Models' wheel well set will be a big help here when it comes available.

As with most old 1/32nd scale models, this kit can be the starting point for an excellent model. But the detailing just isn't there, so a lot of scratchbuilding, or the use of several after-market detailing sets for the cockpit, landing gear, and flaps, is necessary to produce an accurate scale model.

More Detail and Scale Titles from squadron/signal publications....

8248 SBD Dauntless

8250 P-51 Mustang Part 1

8251 P-51 Mustang Part 2

8252 SB2C Helldiver

8253 TBF & TBM Avenger

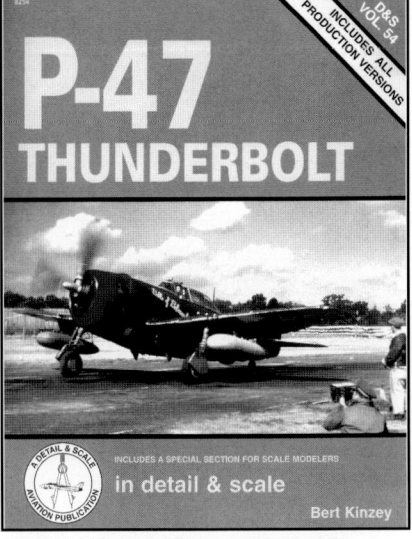

8254 P-47 Thunderbolt